UNDERSTANDING AND RESPONSE

assignments in creative comprehension

Mike Hamlin

Hutchinson

London Melbourne Auckland Johannesburg

Hutchinson Education
An imprint of Century Hutchinson Ltd
62–65 Chandos Place, London WC2N 4NW

Century Hutchinson Australia Pty Ltd
PO Box 496, 16–22 Church Street, Hawthorn,
Victoria 3122, Australia

Century Hutchinson New Zealand Limited
PO Box 40–086, Glenfield, Auckland 10,
New Zealand

Century Hutchinson South Africa (Pty) Ltd
PO Box 337, Bergvlei 2012, South Africa

First published 1988
© Mike Hamlin, 1988

Filmset by Deltatype Ellesmere Port
Printed and bound in Great Britain

British Library Cataloguing in Publication Data

Hamlin, Mike
  Understanding and response: assignments
  in creative comprehension.
  1. English language—Examinations,
  questions, etc.
  I. Title
  428.2   PE1112

  ISBN 0–09–172954–8

Contents

Introduction 5

1 **The Parents' Evening** by Nigel Hinton 7
2 **When I Was ___** by Michael Rosen 12
3 **Flash-Point** (Part One) by Roger Parkes 14
4 **Robot On The Rampage** by James Morrow and Murray Suid 21
5 **Flash-Point** (Part Two) by Roger Parkes 25
6 **Crossing Over** by Catherine Storr 30
7 **Society's Girl** by Christine Bell 34
8 **At the Disco** by Barry Hines 35
9 **First Date** by David Williams 40
10 **Manwatching** by Georgia Garrett 48
11 **After a Quarrel** by John Richmond 49
12 **Listen to Gran?** by Robert Leeson 50
13 **Gregory's Girl — The Cookery Class** by Bill Forsyth, Andrew Bethell and Gerald Cole 55
14 **At The Hairdressers — A Work Experience Diary** by Karen Blakey 61
15 **Diary of a Professional Footballer** by Eamon Dunphy 67
16 **Easy on the Relish** by Andrew Bethell 75
17 **Over Breakfast** by Toeckey Jones 81
18 **A Polished Performance** by D J Enright 86
19 **The Distant One** by Michael Anthony 88
20 **Always in the News** by Posy Simmonds 92
21 **Gutter Press** by Paul Dehn 94
22 **Samuel** by Grace Paley 97
23 **Judgement on Judge Dredd** by John Wagner and Ron Smith 101
24 **Next Term We'll Mash You** by Penelope Lively 104
25 **Five Go Mad in Dorset** by The Comic Strip 110
   The Five are All Together Again by Enid Blyton 111
26 **When the Wind Blows** by Raymond Briggs 116
27 **The Forest on the Superhighway** by Italo Calvino 122
28 **Remote House** by Hans Magnus Enzensberger 126
29 **Golden Girls** by Louise Page 128
30 **Just Visiting** by Dee Phillips 134
31 **Interruption at the Opera House** by Brian Patten 138
32 **Twelve Hours** by Adèle Geras 140
33 **The Little Pet** by Dan Jacobson 147
34 **Remember** by Alice Walker 155
Answers 157

Acknowledgements

The Publishers' thanks are due to the following for permission to reproduce copyright material:
1: J M Dent & Sons Ltd for 'The Parents' Evening' from *Buddy* by Nigel Hinton; 2:
Macmillan, London and Basingstoke for 'When I was 15' by Michael Rosen, from *Speaking
to You* by Rosen and Jackson; 3: Edward Arnold for extracts from *Them and Us* by Roger
Parkes; 4: Boynton Cook Publishers Inc for 'Robot on the Rampage' from *Moviemaking
Illustrated, the Comic Filmbook* by James Morrow and Murray Suid; 6: Faber and Faber Ltd
for 'Crossing Over' from *Cold Marble and Other Short Stories* by Catherine Storr; 7: Sheba
for 'Society's Girl' by Christine Bell from *True to Life* edited by Susan Hemmings; 8:
Michael Joseph Ltd for an extract from *Looks and Smiles* by Barry Hines; 9: David Williams
for 'First Date' from *Love and Marriage* edited by David Self, published by Hutchinson
Education; 10: Georgia Garrett for 'Manwatching' from *Yesterday, Today, Tomorrow*
published by ILEA; 11: John Richmond for 'After a Quarrel' from *Yesterday, Today,
Tomorrow* published by ILEA; 12: William Collins Sons & Co Ltd for an extract from *It's
My Life* © Robert Leeson 1980; 13: Cambridge University Press for Scene 6 from *Gregory's
Girl* by Bill Forsyth, Andrew Bethell and Gerald Cole and W H Allen for extracts from
Gregory's Girl by Bill Forsyth, Andrew Bethell and Gerald Cole; 14: *Times Education
Supplement*, 2nd November 1984, for 'At the Hairdresser's – A Work Experience Diary' by
Karen Blakey; 15: Penguin Books Ltd for an extract from *Only a Game* by Eamon Dunphy,
edited by Peter Ball, published by Kestrel Books in 1976, © Eamon Dunphy and Peter Ball,
1976; 16: Cambridge University Press for Scene 1 from *Easy on the Relish* by Andrew
Bethell; 17: The Bodley Head for an extract from *Go Well, Stay Well* by Toeckey Jones; 18:
Watson, Little Ltd for 'A Polished Performance' by D J Enright from *Collected Poems,*
published by Oxford University Press; 19: Andre Deutsch for 'The Distant One' by Michael
Anthony from *Cricket in the Road* by Michael Anthony; 20: A D Peters & Co Ltd for the
cartoon strip 'Always in the News' by Posy Simmonds, published in the *Guardian* of 2nd
February 1987; 21: Paul Dehn for 'The Fern on the Rock' from *Gutter Press*, published by
Hamish Hamilton; 22: Andre Deutsch for 'Samuel' by Grace Paley from *Enormous
Changes at the Last Minute;* 23: Fleetway Publications Ltd for extracts from *Judge Dredd* by
John Wagner and Ron Smith; 24: Murray Pollinger for 'Next Term We'll Mash You' by
Penelope Lively from *Nothing Missing but the Samovar;* 25: Methuen London for an extract
from 'Five Go Mad in Dorset' from *The Comic Strip Presents* by Richardson and Richens
and Darrell Waters Limited for 'The Five Are All Together Again' by Enid Blyton from *The
Five on Finniston Farm,* 1960; 26: Hamish Hamilton for an extract from *When the Wind
Blows* by Raymond Briggs, Snowman Enterprises Ltd for an extract from the playscript
When the Wind Blows, © 1983 Raymond Briggs/Snowman Enterprises Ltd and Times
Newspapers Ltd, 1987, for the article 'Teachers risk being sued over cartoon' by Sheila
Gunn, which appeared in *The Times* of 17th February 1987; 27: Martin Secker & Warburg
Limited for 'The Forest on the Superhighway' by Italo Calvino from *Marcovaldo*; 28:
Martin Secker & Warburg Limited for 'Remote House' by Hans Magnus Enzensberger,
translated by Michael Hamberger, from *Poems for People Who Don't Read Poems;* 29:
Louise Page for an extract from the playscript *Golden Girls;* 30: Artellus Limited for an
extract from *No, Not I* by Dee Phillips, published by Hodder & Stoughton; 31: Allen &
Unwin for 'Interruption at the Opera House' from *The Irrelevant Song;* 32:
Laura Cecil for 'Twelve Hours' from *More to Life than Mr Right* by Adèle Geras, published
by Piccadilly Press; 33: A M Heath for 'The Little Pet' by Dan Jacobson from *A Way of Life*,
published by Longman; 34: David Higham for 'Remember' by Alice Walker from *Horses
Make a Landscape More Beautiful.*
The Publishers have made every effort to clear copyrights and trust that their apologies will
be accepted for any errors or omissions. They will be pleased to hear from any copyright
holder who has not received due acknowledgement, though where no reply was received to
their letters requesting permission, the Publishers have assumed that there was no objection
to their using the material.

Introduction

Whichever words are used — 'directed response', 'close reading and response', 'understanding and appreciation' — a form of assessment based on an understanding and response to literary, expressive or imaginative writing remains a central examination requirement in both 'English' and 'English Literature', common to all Boards.

Coursework-based schemes of assessment are similarly expected to demonstrate: 'close reading and informed response' or 'evidence of the candidate's ability to understand what he or she has read'.

This book takes the understanding and response to literary or expressive texts as its starting point. Other books will deal with explicitly informational or non-literary material. The aim here is to focus on a wide range of attractive creative writing which, by its very nature, invites a variety of alternative responses. Far from being a limitation, this is a chance to demonstrate the primary strength of literary material; for if chosen well, such material should spontaneously offer space for individual or group contestation and debate.

Based on a selection of stories, playscripts, visual materials and poems, which are worth spending time on, this book will suggest ways in which:

● Response can be *opened out* . Rather than being restricted and limited through long lists of over-literal questions, student response can be developed by five or six key tasks, capable of building interest and widening enquiry.

● Students can begin to *make sense for themselves* ; by introducing their own ideas and insights and testing them out against texts which are capable of answering back.

● A more *reflective reading* can be encouraged; whereby first impressions are used as starting points both for further investigations and for more sustained written responses.

● A more *active relationship* can be established with the text. Replacing mere passivity and point scoring with a generous spirit of interrogation and enquiry.

● *Collaborative work* may be appropriate. Not just as an end in itself but also as a stage in an individual's appreciation of a text.

● Structures and strategies for *productive small group talk* can be encouraged; providing a series of coherent frameworks for oral exploration and debate.

Throughout the book it is intended that the 'understanding assignments' recommended will be flexible enough to fulfil a variety of roles for both 'English' and 'English Literature': whether as preparation for written examination papers, as coursework assignments in their own right, or as guidelines for group discussion and oral assessment.

An approximate 'incline of difficulty' has also been built-in, with the book steadily progressing from immediately accessible texts towards those demanding a deeper consideration and breadth of response.

The Author

Mike Hamlin is an experienced teacher of English in colleges and schools. Currently Head of English and Communication at Greenwood Dale Comprehensive, Nottingham, he is also a Chief Examiner for English GCSE with the Northern Examining Association. He is the author of *Steps in Understanding*, Books 1, 2 & 3 (Hutchinson, 1987) and (with David Jackson) of *Making Sense of Comprehension* (Macmillan, 1984).

1

The PARENTS" EVENING

by NIGEL HINTON

It took Buddy nearly all evening to pluck up the courage to speak to his dad.

'A Parent's what?'

'Consultation Evening. On Friday.'

5 'What they want me for? You in trouble?'

'No. All the parents go. They just say how I've been getting on in all the subjects.'

'What's the matter with reports? That's what we used to 'ave at my school.'

10 'I wish they still had them.'

'I've never 'ad to go before.'

'Mum always used to go. It's nothing, honest. We just sit down and they say what I've done in the term.'

'We? Are you there an' all?'

15 'Of course I am — it's about me, isn't it?'

'Sounds daft to me. What time Friday?'

'Seven-fifteen.'

'Well, I might manage it, I suppose. I'll 'ave to go straight off after.'

20 His dad signed the reply slip and Buddy didn't know whether he was pleased or not. He'd half hoped that his dad would say no and make up a good excuse. The thought of sitting there while his dad made all kinds of mistakes in front of Mr Normington was awful. On the other hand, he was glad that he didn't have to tell Mr Normington

25 that nobody was coming.

The PARENTS' EVENING

Buddy thought he was going to die when his dad came downstairs ready to go at six-thirty. He was dressed in his complete Teddy Boy outfit — drainpipe trousers, drape jacket with velvet collar, bootlace tie, thick crepe-soled shoes and fluorescent green
30 socks. His hair was slicked back with oil and it was obvious that he'd taken great care to look as tidy as possible. He'd dressed himself in his 'best' for the occasion.

'I thought you had to go straight out afterwards,' Buddy said, not daring to come to the point but hoping his dad might change his mind
35 and put on something else. Jeans — anything would be better than this.

'I am. Got me other stuff in 'ere,' he said, holding up a Woolworth's plastic bag.

Buddy's stomach turned to water and he felt sick. The evening
40 was going to be a disaster. 'Dad,' he said weakly.

'What?'

'Can't you put something else on?'

'Why?'

'Well, it's just . . . Mr Normington . . . won't like it.'
45 'He'll 'ave to lump it then, won't he?' There was defiance in his dad's voice but a touch of sadness, too, and Buddy knew he'd hurt him.

The walk to school seemed to take ages. His dad was right. What did it matter what Mr Normington thought? It wasn't as if his dad
50 looked scruffy or dirty — he looked really smart. But he did look different. Even some of the people in the street looked twice as they walked past.

They arrived at the school just after ten past seven. There were pupils and parents all over the school and Buddy led the way to his
55 classroom feeling as if everyone was looking at him. He tried to stay a couple of steps ahead of his dad — not too far to let his dad know it, but enough so that people couldn't be sure they were together.

There were some chairs outside the classroom and his dad sat down while Buddy peeped through the window into the room. Colin
60 Franks was sitting with his well-dressed parents talking to Mr Normington who was wearing a dark suit with a small red rose-bud in the buttonhole.

'It's not bad 'ere, is it?' his dad said and Buddy noticed that he was playing with the plastic bag and looking up and down the
65 corridor, almost as if he were nervous. Buddy watched out of the corner of his eye as his dad brushed the collar of his jacket and

touched the edges of his hair to make sure that it was still tidy. He wiped his hands on his trousers and then checked his nails.

'What's this Mr Normington like, then? All right, is he?'

70 That did it. His dad was scared. Mr Normington would have to lump it. He loved his dad and he didn't care who knew it. He sat down beside him and began telling him about the new block they were in — when it was built, the number of rooms, how they'd found cracks in the ceiling already — anything to stop his dad being scared.

75 The door opened and the Franks came out and walked off down the corridor without even glancing in the direction of Buddy and his dad.

'Next please,' Mr Normington called.

Buddy took a deep breath and led the way in.

80 Mr Normington was standing behind the desk. Buddy saw the eyebrows flicker and the smile freeze as he caught sight of his dad's clothes. There was a brief silence then Mr Normington pulled himself together.

'Ah, Mr Clark. How do you do?' He held his hand out and

85 Buddy's dad went to shake it with the hand holding the plastic bag. He laughed nervously, put the bag down on Mr Normington's desk then shook hands.

'Pleased to meet you.'

'Yes, well . . . Do sit down, Mr Clark, and you, Buddy. Right,

90 where shall we begin? The reports first, perhaps. Oh.' Mr Normington found that all his papers were under the plastic bag. Buddy leaped up and pulled the bag away and Mr Normington began reading the comments that each of the teachers had made. Buddy was so tense that he barely listened, though he was dimly aware that they all

95 sounded quite good. After every subject report Mr Normington stopped and looked at Buddy's dad who kept saying, 'Oh — nice.'

'Well,' Mr Normington said, pushing aside the reports, 'as you can see from those comments, Buddy is doing very well in 3E. We're very pleased with him.'

100 'Oh — nice.'

'Of course, it's a long way off yet, but we're hoping for great things from him in GCSEs.'

'Oh — nice.'

'Have you talked about careers yet?'

105 Buddy's dad glanced at him with a slightly worried look, so Buddy butted in, 'Well, we've talked about some things but I haven't made up my mind yet.'

'Of course. I'm sorry, Mr Clark,' Mr Normington said, looking down at Buddy's record card, 'I can't recall what you do for a living.'

110 Buddy's heart raced.

'Ah, yes — here it is. Oh, you worked at Bradley's. That's closed down, hasn't it?'

'Yeah, beginning of the year. I do a bit with antiques on the side now. I'm 'oping to start a shop like what I used to 'ave.'

115 Buddy winced at the dropped 'h's but Mr Normington nodded and smiled.

'Well, then,' he said, 'I don't think there's much else from our end. Unless, of course, you've got any problems at your end?'

'No, everyfink's fine,' his dad said quickly.

120 'Good. Good. Well, let's hope young Buddy keeps up the good work. Make sure you always supervise his prep, etcetera.'

'Prep?' his dad said, and darted a look at Buddy.

'Yes, private studies — in the evenings,' Mr Normington said.

Understanding

1   After reading the first 19 lines, write down all the evidence you can find which convinces you that Buddy's father is not keen on attending the 'Consultation Evening'.

2   Read lines 20–25. Why didn't Buddy know whether he was pleased or not? What contrasting thoughts were going through his mind?

3   Lines 45–47 read: 'There was defiance in his dad's voice but a touch of sadness, too, and Buddy knew he'd hurt him.' Now read again lines 26–47. Why do you think his father might have been hurt by Buddy's remarks and attitude?

4   Buddy and his father arrive at the school (lines 53–62). Describe as best you can Buddy's thoughts and feelings as he looks around him.

5   Several things happen (lines 63–71), which suggest that Buddy's father is anxious as he waits for Mr Normington. Write down as many as you can find, adding your own comments on the words and phrases used.

'Oh, 'omework. Oh yes, he's good like that — always does it.'

125 'Not too much time wasted in front of the television?'

'We 'aven't got a telly. We . . . er . . . got rid of it.'

'Did you?' Mr Normington said, and Buddy could see he was impressed. 'Good. There's some splendid stuff on it, of course — but it can be a dreadful time-waster. Well, well — thank you for coming,

130 Mr Clark.'

They all stood up and Buddy's dad shook hands with Mr Normington.

'By the way, how's Mrs Clark? Well, I trust.'

'Oh, yeah — she's ok.'

135 'Good. Give her my regards.'

'Yeah, I will.'

As they walked to the door, Buddy could almost feel the relief pouring off his dad.

---

6   **Either:**
     (a) As Buddy and his father walk home they talk about the 'Consultation' they have just had with Mr Normington. What would they say to each other?

     Or:
     (b) After the 'Consultation Evening', Mr Normington joins other teachers for a coffee in the staff-room. He describes his meeting with Buddy and his father. What would he say?

Response

1   Write about a parents' consultation evening which you can remember. You may wish to describe some of the preparations for the evening as well as your thoughts and feelings while the interviews were taking place.

2   Write about a time, real or imagined, when you have felt embarrassed at being seen with a parent. You may like to write about one of those 'awkward' moments when you are out with your parents and you meet some of your friends from school — what would happen?

2

WHEN I

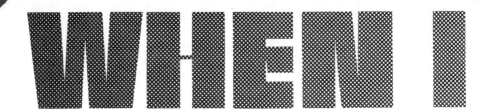

Ken said to me,
'You know your trouble,
you don't hold your bag right.'
'What's wrong with it?' I said.
'It's not so much the way you hold it -
It's the way you put it down.
You've got to look at it as if you ■ ■
Watch me.'

He went out
he walked back in
shoulders back
elbows out
bag balanced in his hand.

'Watch me.'

He stopped walking.
His arm froze
and the bag flew out of his hand
as if he'd kicked it.
He didn't even ■ at it.
'Now you try,' he said.
'I'll show you where you've gone wrong.'
I went out the door,
I rambled back in again with my bag.
I stopped walking
My arm froze — just like his,
but the bag fell out of my hand
and flopped on to the floor
like a ■ ■

'Useless,' he said.
'You don't convince — that's your trouble.'
'So?' I said.
'I'm a slob. I can't change that.'
I didn't say that I *would* try and change
in case that would show I was giving in to him.

But ■
on my own,
in my room,
in front of the mirror
I spent hours and hours
practising bag-dropping.
Walking in,
freeze the arm,
let the bag drop.
Walk in
arm freeze
bag drop.
Again and again
till I thought I had got it right.

I don't suppose any girl noticed.
I don't suppose any girl ever
    said to herself,
'I love the way he drops his
    bag . . .'

by Michael Rosen

Understanding

1   After you have read through this poem several times, list some possibilities for the seven 'gaps' which are there, including the one in the title! Start by writing down several possibilities for each 'gap', but finally, select the word or words that seem to fit best in terms of sound and meaning. Give reasons for your final selection of 'gap' fillers.

2   In verse two, a certain way of walking is being described. Who else would walk like this? Try to picture it in your mind's eye for a moment, then write down some possibilities along with your reasons for choosing them.

3   Verse four describes Michael Rosen's attempt at walking in with his bag. In what ways does this differ from the description mentioned above? What is there in his choice of words or style of writing which helps to create this very different impression?

4   Verse five gives a reader some clues as to the type of boy Michael Rosen was. How would you describe the kind of behaviour mentioned here? What sort of person would behave in this way?

5   The last three lines (verse six), provide a final comment on the boy, and the whole incident with Ken and the bag. What conclusions are being drawn here? Why do you think this?

Response

1   'How to hold a bag' might well be crucially important at a certain age, but what might be the next obstacle to 'super cool' perfection? After thinking through some possibilities — how to be 'seen' at a disco, choosing just the right clothes, talking about the latest music — write a poem of your own which attempts to capture just such a moment. Use a style similar to Michael Rosen's if it helps you to get started.

13

flash-point

Roger Parkes
PART ONE

Fade into end of chemistry practical. The rest of the 5th year class are leaving the lab as **Trevor,** *who is on report, goes to collect his card from* **Miss Frinton.**

Trevor	My report card, Miss.
Frinton	Oh yes.
Carol	(*calls*) Hey, Trev . . .
Trevor	Just coming.
Frinton	There you are.
Trevor	(*reading her comment*) 'Noisy and inattentive.' That's not fair!
Carol	(*in warning*) Trevor . . .
Frinton	(dismissive) If you want good reports, do your homework, write up your experiments, and *try* instead of always shouting and showing off.
Trevor	I *do* try!
Frinton	Rubbish. Constantly disruptive. You only started chemistry at all because Carol's doing it.
Trevor	(*sulky*) Didn't . . .
Carol	(*brightly*) He's okay really, Miss.
Frinton	Then he can show it, Carol, by revising and doing well in the mocks next week. (**Trevor** *and* **Carol** *leave, talking together as they go to the next class.*)
Carol	You want to watch out with her.
Trevor	Flaming Flash-point!
Carol	You and her both, Trev. Sharp tongues and quick tempers.

Trevor	(*snorts in contempt*) She's just looking for trouble.
Carol	Well don't you be the one to give it her or she'll have you out.
Trevor	Out where?
Carol	Out the school, you wallie, quick as light.
Trevor	You think that's what she's aiming at?
Carol	Could be. (*she shrugs*) Mind you, Trev, you do wind her up.

Fade to chemistry lab after the mocks. This time **Miss Frinton** *and* **Trevor** *are alone.*

Frinton	I'm sorry, Trevor, but that's final.
Trevor	(*angry*) But that's not . . .
Frinton	(*interrupting*) Your results in the mocks show you don't stand a chance of getting a grade in the GCSE exam. There is no point in you entering for it.
Trevor	(*fiddling with one of the gas-taps*) But look . . .
Frinton	(*interrupting*) Leave that gas-tap alone. You know you're not supposed to touch them.
Trevor	But I really need to have chemistry . . .
Frinton	(*interrupting*) Too late to think of that now.
Trevor	But . . .
Frinton	(*persisting*) You should have done some revision.
Trevor	(*again his hand goes to the gas-tap*) I did revise . . .
Frinton	Will you stop fiddling with that gas-tap! *Now.* (*She hits irritably at his hand.*)
Trevor	(*explosive*) Get off! don't touch me again! *Ever*!

Fade to **Trevor's** *home that evening.*

Mrs Wade	But, Trevor, if you're going in for photography, you're going to need a pass in chemistry. I'm sure the careers master said . . .
Trevor	(*interrupting*) Look, mum, whether I need it or not, there's no chance now. Orders of Ober-Sturm-Fuehrer Flashpoint. Verbotten! Finito!
	Pause.
Trevor	Not a hope.
Mrs Wade	But why?
Trevor	Old Frinton's got the knife out for me, that's why.
Mrs Wade	What?

Trevor	Carol reckons she's trying to get me the boot.
Mrs Wade	(*alarmed*) From Oakleigh? But why?
Trevor	Vendetta, that's why. She has her favourites — the swots like Don Green and them — and her pet hates like me. I'm just a write-off to her. Just dole-queue junk.

Fade to chemistry practical the next week.

Frinton	Trevor Wade, will you go and work where I told you.
Trevor	But Ronnie and me always go together.
Frinton	(*firm*) Not today. This acid experiment is too risky for me to be constantly keeping an eye on you.
Trevor	We'll be careful.
Frinton	No, I want you with someone reliable. Now go and work with Donald like I told you. (*Pause.*) Now I want all of you to remember how dangerous acid can be. You do *not* warm it over the bunsen burner the way Jenny's just started to do so. Hold on, Jenny, I'll just come and . . . (**Miss Frinton** *checks, realising* **Trevor** *has moved again.*) Trevor, for the *second* time, go and work with Donald!
Trevor	Look, I just want to talk to . . .
Frinton	Back over there. *Now.* (*Pause.*) Firstly, Jenny, use the tube-holder so you don't drop the test-tube when it gets hot. Now then, just watch . . .
Trevor	(*quietly to* **Donald**) Let's have that test-tube.
Donald	What?
Trevor	(*snatching it*) Give it here.
Donald	What are you doing? Hey you've broken it!
Trevor	(*calling out*) Miss! Breakage, Miss!
Frinton	(*to* **Jenny**) See how I keep the open end angled safely away so that, if the acid does spurt up . . .
Trevor	(*calls*) *Miss!*
Carol	Trev wants you, Miss.
Frinton	Just watch what I'm doing, Carol. Forget about Trevor Wade.
Trevor	(*calls*) Miss, I've broken me thingy! (*He climbs up on his lab stool and starts aping about.*)
Donald	Stop it, Trevor. Get down, you wallie!
Trevor	Shut up, you.
Frinton	(*calls*) Get down, Trevor.

Janet	(*interrupting*) Some more acid please, Miss.
Frinton	Stay at your place, Janet, I'll bring it over.
Trevor	(*calls*) Can't manage without me thingy, Miss!
Frinton	Get down off that stool, Trevor.
Jenny	You need to *shout* at him, Miss.
Frinton	(*moving towards him*) Trevor, get *down* . . . (*She emphasises the command by waving angrily at him with her free hand.* **Trevor** *reacts, lurching back with an indignant cry.*)
Trevor	Hey! (*He swings his arms wildly around to keep from falling, one hand striking the teacher violently across the side of the face.* **Miss Frinton** *lurches heavily back against the nearest lab bench. The acid bottle breaks against it, splashing her with acid as she goes down on the floor.*)
Trevor	Watch out! (*He clambers off the stool, going to her.*) Here, you okay?
Frinton	Monster! Get back!
Trevor	But . . .
Frinton	*Back!*
Donald	Watch out for all that acid!
Janet	I'll fetch Mrs James.
Carol	Here, that's blood!
Jenny	She's all cut, look.
Donald	I'll help you, Miss.
Frinton	I'll manage. Just run lots of water to swamp all this spilt acid.
Jack	What happened?
Jenny	He hit her.
Trevor	Just — an *accident* . . .
Donald	*Liar* . . .
Trevor	*It was!* Carol, you saw.
Carol	That's right, yeah. An accident.
Frinton	Jack, go and get Mrs McKendrick. Quick as you can.
Donald	You're still bleeding, Miss.
Frinton	Yes, it'll need stitching.
Mrs James	Good heavens, what happened?
Frinton	Trevor Wade hit me. Knocked me over.

Fade to head's office next morning.

Mrs Wade	Suspended?
Head	For the time being, yes.

Mrs Wade	Outrageous. You have no right.
Head	An assault on a teacher, Mrs Wade. Extremely serious.
Mrs Wade	Except that it was an *accident.* Right, Trevor?
Trevor	Yeah — definitely.
Head	I'm fully aware of Trevor's version.
Mrs Wade	Not just Trevor's. I've talked to his classmates. They all confirm it.
Head	Mrs Wade, Trevor is suspended until the special meeting of the panel next week and that is final.
Mrs Wade	*She pushed him!* That Frinton woman hit him to get him down off the stool. She's the one who ought to be suspended, not Trevor! *Pause.*
Head	Mrs Wade, your son's past record of indiscipline . . .
Mrs Wade	(*interrupting*) That's not proof of anything. I insist you take him back. Now. *Pause.*
Head	Well if so, there'll have to be an independent investigation by the police — who just might decide to prosecute.
Mrs Wade	What?
Head	It's your decision.

Fade to police station next day. A police constable interviewing **Trevor** *while his mother listens.*

Constable	Once again, please, Trevor, to make sure I've got the details down right. Start from where you broke the test-tube.
Trevor	Okay, it's one of her rules in chemi prac: if you break anything you have to report it straight away. She's supposed to come over, see how it got broken and that. But when I started calling her, she took no notice.
Constable	And that's when you got up on the stool?
Trevor	Well yeah — to catch her attention.
Constable	(*writing it down*) To catch her attention.
Trevor	You see, because it was *me* calling, she had to go and make out she hadn't heard. Typical. See, she's got it in for me and . . .
Constable	(*interrupting*) Just the facts, please. What happened next?

Trevor	Well, at last she started across, but instead of asking what's up, she yelled at me to *get down* and took this great shove at me. Took me by surprise — caught me off balance. Okay, next thing, she dodged back and clobbered into the bench.
Constable	Yes?
Trevor	Well, she was holding this acid bottle and it got smashed. Cut her hand — acid all over the place. So naturally I nipped down to help her. But, well, she pushed me away. Called me a mad animal or something.
Constable	Oh? Why should she do that, Trevor, if it all happened the way you just said?

Fade to school, **Trevor** *and* **Carol** *talking to* **Donald Green.**

Donald	(*surprised*) Flippin heck, I didn't know the police were onto it.
Trevor	They wouldn't have been except the head goon wanted to blame me — making out I *meant* to hit her. Anyway, it's no sweat because everyone else saw it wasn't like that — saw it was an accident.
Donald	Oh. Well — er . . .
Carol	Of course it was, Donald. You saw old Flash-point shove him.
Donald	I didn't think she actually touched you, Trevor.
Trevor	Of course she did. Why else should I swing around like that?
Donald	You see, I thought . . .
Carol	Yeah? What?
Donald	Well, that Trevor was pretending — putting that on.
Trevor	*Why?* What was there to pretend about?
Donald	Er . . .
Trevor	She shoved me — made me lose my balance. Okay? *Pause.*
Donald	If you say so.
Trevor	You say so, too, Donald old son. There's no sense any of us telling it differently to the police.
Donald	Oh.
Carol	Of course there isn't, you whimp. *Pause.*

FLASH POINT Part One

Trevor	Okay then? Accident?
	Pause.
Donald	Okay.
Trevor	Right. Same as the way that test-tube got broken.
Donald	What?
Carol	Maybe you didn't see how it happened.
Donald	Yes I did. Trev took it from me and . . .
Trevor	(*interrupting*) Dropped it by accident.
Donald	Oh.
Trevor	(*menacing*) I don't think you did see it, old son. Okay?
Donald	(*after a pause*) Okay.

Understanding

Fade to courtroom . . .

1   The next scene begins with Miss Frinton giving evidence and being cross-examined by a lawyer. She is then followed into the witness box by Trevor, Carol and Donald. From what you know of the play so far, take each character in turn and write the exchange that you think would take place between these four witnesses and the lawyer. How would their attitudes and evidence differ?

2   The final scene involves the magistrate deciding on Trevor's guilt or innocence. Write down your prediction of the most likely outcome.

Now turn to Flash-Point *(Part Two) on page 25.*

ROBOT ON THE RAMPAGE

by James Morrow and Murray Suid

Shooting scripts are attempts to describe in words a story or sequence of events which is intended to be shown, visually, through a series of images or pictures. They are frequently used as starting points for film and video productions but they can also help to plan comic strip or cartoon sequences, allowing a writer to explain in detail precisely what he or she wants from an illustrator. What follows is an example of this second type of shooting script.

EXTERIOR LIGHTHOUSE — CLOSE-UP — DAY

1. Fade-in on robot staring straight ahead.

> **ROBOT**
> I have forgotten one important fact!
> I do not *have* to get in! Soon, *he*
> will come out to *me!*

EXTERIOR LIGHTHOUSE — LONG-SHOT — DAY

2. Establishing shot with the camera behind the robot. He is on the left, gesturing with one arm. A lighthouse is on the right, slightly in the background.

> **ROBOT**
> I will waste no more energy! I will
> simply wait here, without sleeping,
> until you unbolt the door!

> **LIGHTHOUSE KEEPER**
> Never! I'll *never* open the door!

INTERIOR LIGHTHOUSE — MID-SHOT — DAY

3. A slight high-angle of the keeper, who is in the foreground, facing forward. The robot can be seen through the window, gesturing as in Shot 2.

ROBOT

Have you forgotten that your *food* is
out here? And your supply of drinking
water? Without them, you *perish!*

KEEPER (voice-over)

He's right! He could *starve* me out in
a matter of hours! And then . . . who would
tend the beacon?

EXTERIOR LIGHTHOUSE — LONG-SHOT — DAY

4. Jump cut to the robot sitting on an old wooden box, facing the
   lighthouse.

NARRATOR (voice-over)

And so the long hours pass, as the robot, needing no rest, no food,
sits and waits . . . never relaxing his vigil . . .

ROBOT

You have no choice, human! You *must*
come out for food — or else you
perish! Perhaps I will be merciful . . .
Perhaps I shall allow you to live long
enough to watch the 'Superba' crash
among the rocks!

Understanding

1   Look carefully at how the first four frames of this comic strip story are described in the shooting script which accompanies it. The strip then continues for a further ten frames, the shooting script, however, does not! Work through those remaining ten frames, describing them in exactly the same way as those first four frames were described to you. That is:

(a) Start each frame description with a bold outline of where the action is taking place — inside or outside; the type of shot being used — close-up, mid-shot, long shot etc., plus whether it is day or night.

(b) Describe the shot in more detail: whether a visual angle is being used; what is in the foreground or background of the frame; what the various characters are doing etc.

(c) Make sure the words spoken are written out as in a playscript, with the speaker named and any emphasis or stress indicated.

2   Now compare your shooting script with the original, which you can find on page 158. List any differences between the two scripts and comment on any interesting disagreements.

3   You may well have guessed from the visual style of the comic that it is an American strip cartoon; but it is also a strip with a message, which does not become clear until the final frame. Using your own words, what 'message' does this strip seem to be arguing for?

4   Without necessarily agreeing or disagreeing with this message, how successful would you say this strip is in getting its central idea across to a wide audience? Give reasons for your answer.

Response

1   Choose a comic strip of your own and, by considering each frame carefully, attempt to 'work backwards' towards its original shooting script. Set it out in a similar way to 'Robot on the Rampage'.

2   Alternatively, create a new shooting script of your own, either with a view to illustrating it yourself later or, if you are lucky, getting someone else to draw it for you!

flash-point

Roger Parkes
Part Two

Fade to courtroom. **Miss Frinton** *is giving evidence.*

Frinton	I again ordered him off the stool and then gestured. He gave this wild bellow and struck out at me — hit me across the side of the face — knocked me completely off balance. Then he jumped down and, just for a moment, I thought he was going to hit me again. But then — well I think he began to realise what he'd done — my cuts, all the blood, the acid and soforth.
Lawyer	Miss Frinton, you say you gestured. Might you have *touched* him when you did that?
Frinton	Definitely not, no.
Lawyer	Is it true you are known to your pupils as Flash-point?
Frinton	(*frowns*) So I've heard.
Lawyer	Do you know why that might be?
Frinton	To do with practicals on hydrocarbons, I imagine. When we measure their various flashpoints.
Lawyer	Oh? Nothing to do with your temperament? (*Pause.* **Miss Frinton** *shrugs but stays silent.*)
Lawyer	(*continues*) You see, I'm asking if this incident really happened in quite the way you've described.
Frinton	It did.

Lawyer	You had a tricky experiment to oversee, you saw Trevor call to you from up on his lab stool; and you reached, er, flashpoint, yes? You shouted at him to get down and then you enforced it by giving him a push . . .
Frinton	No. He hit me. Quite deliberately — as I just said.
Lawyer	It isn't that, through your dislike of Trevor Wade, your memory is playing you false?
Frinton	No. I wrote it all down that same day in the Accident Book, so I'm quite certain.

Fade to later— **Trevor** *now in the witness box.*

Lawyer	Trevor, how did the test-tube get broken?
Trevor	Can't remember.
Lawyer	When you got up on the stool, wasn't it really because you wanted to put on an act?
Trevor	You what?
Lawyer	To amuse your mates.
Trevor	No. I was trying to get her attention about the breakage.
Lawyer	Well I suggest you were up there solely to lark about.
Trevor	No.
Lawyer	And when Miss Frinton ignored these absurd antics of yours, you saw that it would mean losing face in front of your mates.
Trevor	I don't understand . . .
Lawyer	Wasn't it because of that you suddenly saw red and lashed out at her?
Trevor	*No.* It was an accident, like I said.

Fade to later. **Carol** *is now in the witness box.*

Carol	So then old Flash-point — er, sorry, Miss Frinton — she takes the bottle and goes off to Janet. Okay, just as she's passing Trev, I saw her take this great shove at him — like, to push him down off the stool.
Lawyer	You saw that clearly? An actual push?
Carol	Yeah! Then Miss dodged back against the bench and fell. Then, when Trev nipped down to help her, she yelled at him, making out she was scared, making out he was to blame.
Lawyer	Why ever should she do that?

Carol   Obvious. Because she's got it in for him. She's always picking on him. Real vendetta.

Fade to later. **Donald** *is now in the witness box.*

Lawyer   So, Donald, you thought you saw Miss Frinton push at Trevor, causing him to lose his balance and accidentally hit her, is that it?

Donald   Well, er, yes, I suppose so.

Lawyer   How did the test-tube get broken?

Donald   (*mutters*) Er . . . (**Donald** *glances at* **Trevor** *who shakes his head.*)

Lawyer   Don't look at Trevor now. You are giving evidence to the magistrates, not to him.

Donald   Er, I didn't see how.
Tense pause.

Lawyer   Donald, would you expect the magistrates to be aware of the kind of pressures which youngsters like you and Carol can face from their classmates? From boys they meet everyday in class and hence are obliged to get along with?
Pause. **Donald** *stares in silence.*

Lawyer   (*continues*) Has Trevor Wade ever threatened you?
Pause. **Donald** *is unable to speak.*

Lawyer   (*continues*) Donald, you do realise what it means to be under oath? That lying in this court is an offence just as serious as the one Trevor is charged with?

Donald   (*near to panic*) Yes.

Lawyer   And have you so far been truthful with this court? (*pause*) Might you have twisted your evidence somewhat so as to help a classmate?
Pause. **Donald** *gestures in shame and fear.*

Donald   Yes . . .

Lawyer   Would you like to tell the magistrates again what you remember of the incident?
Donald *nods in relief.*

Donald   You see, to begin with, he was angry with Miss Frinton because she kept sending him back to work with me. So when he came back the second time, he grabbed the test-tube from me and then smashed it. Deliberately. Then he started yelling out to her and waving the broken bits. Next he got

FLASH POINT Part Two

up on his stool and started raving on — showing off as usual. Next thing, Miss Frinton came across, told him to get down and waved at him. But instead he gave this wild yell and acted it up that she'd made him lose his balance. He flung around and hit her on the side of the face.

Fade to later — the magistrates now outside discussing their verdict.

Carol	(*to* **Donald**) Rotten little traitor!
Donald	Shut up!
Trevor	Why'd you say all that?
Donald	What?
Trevor	Trying to drop me in it — saying all that about me acting up.
Donald	You were! As usual!
Trevor	Not about losing my balance. Not then I wasn't!
Donald	Well that's how it looked to me!
Carol	Rubbish!
Donald	Look, Carol, I was stood right beside him. He deliberately made out he was off balance so as to . . .
Trevor	(*interrupting*) It was an accident like I said.
Donald	(*scornful*) Oh yes . . .
Trevor	Yes!
Donald	Well then, why'd you threaten me?
Trevor	You what?
Donald	At school — before I spoke to the police.
Trevor	(guffaws) Who are you kidding . . . (*he stops as the lawyer calls out*).
Lawyer	(*calls*) Stand in court!
	Pause as the three magistrates return.
Lawyer	(*continues*) Trevor, remain standing.

Magistrate   Trevor Neil Wade, we find the case against you proved.

Fade to several weeks later, once again in court.

Magistrate   From the head's report on you, Trevor, we note that you have now been transferred to another school. We very much hope you will use that move as an opportunity to start afresh, keep out of trouble and learn to get on with people. (*Pause*) Now then, because this is your first trouble in court, we shan't be sending you away to a detention centre. Instead we order that you be put on probation for twelve months. Now this isn't a let-off. You'll have to report regularly and comply with the various conditions. If you fail to do so — to the letter — you could be brought back again to the court to be dealt with.

Understanding

After reading the remaining scenes carefully:

1   Taking the four witnesses in turn. How did *each* cross-examination differ from the ones you predicted earlier? Go through each piece of evidence in detail and give your views on any differences you find.

2   How do the final verdicts and sentences compare? Again, explain any differences between your version and the original.

Response

1   After reading and considering the whole play, what thoughts or comments would you now make about its effectiveness as a piece of drama? You could write up your ideas in the form of a review for a school magazine or a local paper.

by Catherine Storr

CROSSING OVER

If she hadn't been fond of dogs, she would never have volunteered
for this particular job. When her class at school were asked if they
would give up some of their spare time towards helping old people,
most of the tasks on offer had sounded dreary. Visiting housebound
5   old men and women, making them cups of tea and talking to them;
she hadn't fancied that, and she wasn't any good at making
conversation, let alone being able to shout loud enough for a deaf
person to hear. Her voice was naturally quiet. She didn't like the idea
of doing anyone else's shopping, she wasn't good enough at
10   checking that she'd got the right change. The check-out girls in the
supermarket were too quick, ringing up the different items on the
cash register. Nor did she want to push a wheelchair to the park. But
walking old Mrs Matthews' dog, that had seemed like something she
might even enjoy. She couldn't go every evening, but she would take
15   him for a good long run on the Common on Saturdays, and on fine
evenings, when the days were longer, she'd try to call for him after
school some weekdays. She had started out full of enthusiasm.

What she hadn't reckoned with was the dog himself. Togo was
huge, half Alsatian, half something else which had given him long
20   woolly hair, permanently matted and dirty. Once, right at the
beginning, she had offered to bathe and groom him, but Mrs
Matthews had been outraged by the suggestion, was sure the poor
creature would catch cold, and at the sight of the comb, Togo backed
and growled and showed his teeth. It was as much as she could do to
25   fasten and unfasten his leash, and he did not make that easy. The
early evening walks weren't quite so bad, because there wasn't time
to take him to the Common, so he stayed on the leash all the time.
Even then he was difficult to manage. He seemed to have had no
training and he certainly had no manners. He never stopped when
30   she told him to, never came when she called him, so that every
Saturday, when she dutifully let him run free among the gorse bushes
and little trees on the Common, she was afraid she might have to
return to Mrs Matthews without the dog, confessing that he had run
away. Mrs Matthews did not admit that Togo was unruly and difficult
35   to manage, any more than she would admit that he smelled. It was
only a feeling that she shouldn't go back on her promise to perform
this small service to the community that kept the girl still at the
disagreeable task.

This particular evening was horrible. She'd been kept later at
40   school than usual, and although it was already March, the sky was

30

overcast, it was beginning to get dark, and a fine drizzling rain made the pavements slippery. Togo was in a worse mood than usual. He had slouched along, stopping for whole minutes at lampposts and dustbins and misbehaving extravagantly in the most inconvenient
45 places, in spite of her frantic tugs at the leash to try to get him off the pavement. He was too strong for her to control, and he knew it. She almost believed that he had a spite against her, and enjoyed showing that he didn't have to do anything she wanted, as if it wasn't bad enough having to go out in public with an animal so unkempt and
50 anti-social.

They reached the zebra crossing on the hill. The traffic was moving fast, as it always did during the evening rush-hour. She would have to wait for a break before she could step off the pavement, especially as, in the half dark, she knew from her Dad's comments
55 when he was driving, pedestrians on the road were not easy to see. She stood still and dragged at Togo's lead. But Togo did not mean to be dictated to by a little schoolgirl, and after a moment's hesitation, he pulled too. He was off, into the middle of the on-coming traffic, wrenching at the leash, which she had twisted round her hand in
60 order to get a better grip. She threw all her weight against his, but she was no match for him. She thought she felt the worn leather snap, she heard the sound of screaming brakes and someone shouted. She had time to think, 'What am I going to say to Mrs Matthews?', before her head swam and she thought she was going to faint.
65 She found herself standing on the further side of the road. She saw a huddle of people, surrounding stationary cars. Two drivers had left their vehicles and were abusing each other. As the crowd swayed, she saw the bonnet of a red car crumpled by its contact with the back of a large yellow van. She saw, too, a dark stain on the road surface.
70 Blood. Blood made her feel sick, and her head swam again. She hesitated, knowing that she ought to go among the watching people to make herself look, perhaps to try to explain how Togo had pulled, how she hadn't been strong enough to hold him back. Someone should be told whose dog he was. Someone would have to go and
75 break the terrible news to Mrs Matthews.

As she was considering this, she heard the siren of a police car and the two-note call of an ambulance. She thought, 'Perhaps someone got badly hurt in one of the cars, and it's all my fault.' Her courage evaporated, and she turned away from the accident and
80 began to walk, on legs that trembled, up the hill towards her own home. She thought, 'I'll go and tell Mum.' But then she remembered how much Mrs Matthews loved horrible Togo, how she talked about him as her only friend, and how dreadful it was going to be for her to open her front door to find a policeman telling her that her dog was
85 dead. Besides, the policeman might say that it was all her, the girl's,

fault. She had to go first to Mrs Matthews' house, to break the news gently, and also to explain that she had tried her best to prevent the accident.

90 She found that she must have been walking really fast, which was surprising, considering how much she was dreading the ordeal in front of her. She had reached the grocer's and the newspaper shop at the top of the High Street almost before she'd realized. She saw Sybil Grainger coming out of the newspaper shop, and she was ready to say, 'Hi!' and to pretend that there was nothing wrong, but luckily

95 Sybil seemed not to have seen her. She turned the corner into Grange Road, relieved that she hadn't had to carry on a conversation. Grange Road also seemed shorter than usual; now she had to go along Fenton Crescent till she reached the small side street where Mrs Matthews lived, in one of the row of little old cottages known as

100 Paradise Row.

Her heart beat furiously as she unlatched the small wooden gate and walked the short distance up to the front door, rehearsing exactly how to say what she had to. She lifted the knocker. As it came down on the wood, it made a hollow, echoing sound.

105 Extraordinary. From the other side of the door, she heard something very much like Togo's deep, menacing growl. She must be in such a state of nerves that she was imagining impossible things. Or perhaps when she felt faint out there in the road, she had fallen and hit her head and been concussed. She felt her scalp, under the

110 straight, silky hair, but she couldn't find any tender spots. She waited. Mrs Matthews was arthritic and always took a long time to answer the door and there was no hurry for the message she was going to receive.

Steps came slowly, dragging a little, along the passage. The door

115 opened, and she braced herself for the shock she was about to administer and the scolding she was certainly going to receive.

But when Mrs Matthews looked out, she behaved in a very peculiar way. Instead of saying immediately, 'Where's Togo?' she asked nothing of her visitor, but bent forward and peered out, looking

120 up and down the short row of cottages, as if she were searching for something or someone who might be coming or going in the street. Her head with its thinning grey hair was so close that the girl stepped back, opening her mouth to begin her explanation. But what she saw in the passage behind the old woman stopped her from uttering a

125 sound.

At the further end of the passage was a dog. Togo. Togo, whole, apparently unharmed, his collar round his neck, and the end of the broken leash still attached, dragging behind him.

For a moment she thought he was going to spring forward and

130 attack her. Then she saw that, instead, he was backing, shrinking as far away as he could get. He was making a curious noise, not a howl, nor a growl, but a sort of whine. She noticed that he was trembling. She had never seen Togo tremble before. He was showing whites round his yellow eyes and the short hair round his muzzle was
135 bristling.

She started to speak. But Mrs Matthews appeared not to have heard her. She was turning back to calm the terrified dog. She was saying, 'Whatever's the matter with you, Togo? Think you're seeing a ghost?'

Understanding

1   What was it about those voluntary jobs which made them sound so 'dreary' to the girl at the beginning of the story? List as many points as you can find.

2   Togo is often mentioned between lines 13 and 38. Using evidence from this section of the story, describe Togo as fully as you can in your own words.

3   Even before the accident, the girl sensed that certain things seemed to be going wrong. What things in particular were worrying the girl and for what reasons?

4   After the accident, no one is quite sure what exactly has happened. Only gradually do you, as a reader, begin to suspect what might have happened to the girl, but even these suspicions are not confirmed until the very last line. Re-read the story from the point of the accident to the end, but as you read through make a list of all the hints, clues and suggestions that lead you towards your final conclusion as to what happened to the girl. How many clues can you find buried away in the story?

Response

1   Ghost stories are not to everyone's taste. However, ordinary, everyday situations can be transformed into the extra-ordinary by the use of such supernatural devices. Choose just such an everyday event — a visit to the hairdressers, a walk in the park, preparing the sandwiches for lunch — and by adding a supernatural twist, transform them into extraordinary happenings!

SOCIETY'S Girl
by Christine Bell

She stares into the looking glass
But she can't see herself.
Maybe she's hiding behind the glass
But she looks and she's not there either
5 What can she see then?
Nothing much apart from a painted face
So perfectly applied as if a piece of precision engineering
Each lash is defined and her brows in attention stand
Her lips move gently, fearing to rub red onto the white stones behind.
10 Her skin stands, as a piece of art
It took so long to make it look so natural.
But where is she?
Hidden perhaps behind her precious image
Daring not to show herself in case they should laugh.
15 They all cry out for this china doll
They all want her to be theirs
'But how can I be theirs if I'm not mine?'
She asks, shaking her head.
The doorbell rings and she puts her thoughts into her tweezer case.
20 Gets out her false smile and leaves her soul behind.

Understanding

1   What is being suggested in the first two lines of this poem? Why can't she 'see herself'?

2   Who do you think 'they' of lines 15 and 16 might be? Why should 'they' matter?

3   Consider line 19. What does the image of her putting 'her thoughts into her tweezer case' suggest to you?

4   Recommend two or three alternative titles that would be suitable for this poem.

Response

1   This poem has the title 'Society's Girl'. Attempt a similarly written poem yourself which considers some of the pressures on boys to behave and perform in certain ways. You could call your poem 'Society's Boy'.

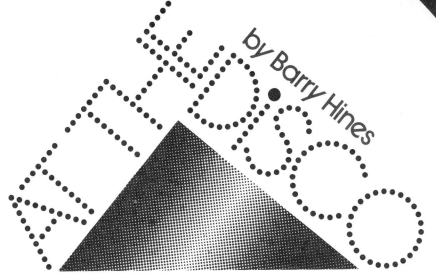

He watched the dancers. There were many different styles. One
group of girls, dancing in a line, had copied their routine from artistes
they had seen on the television. They all faced the same way,
performed the same steps, the same simultaneous turns, the same
5   semaphore movements of the arms. They even smiled together.
They had practised a long time to records at home to become as
skilful as that. Some thought they *were* on the television, or on a film,
or on the stage. They wanted cameras and spotlights on them. They
wanted applause. They wanted the floor cleared so that everybody
10   could watch them. Too cool to sweat, their perspiration polished
them. They were solitary dancers absorbed in their own performance, hoping they had at last found a talent that would make them
into someone else.

     The others just moved around to the music, enjoying themselves
15   and testing their partners with looks and smiles. Then, if the signals
were right, they danced closer together when the disc jockey played a
ballad.

     Mick noticed a girl in a blue dress sitting at a table. She was
laughing at something another girl was saying to her. He could tell it
20   was rude by the way she pretended to look shocked and nudged her
friend to make her shut up. Instead, the other girl whispered
something else and pointed to a boy dancing in front of them. The girl
started to laugh again, and while she was shaking her head in mock
protest, she noticed Mick smiling at her. She was not embarrassed or
25   haughty, as she might have been if she had thought he was trying to
attract her attention. She could tell that he was amused and, because
of this, she was able to smile back.

     They became aware of each other then. The more they tried not
to look at each other, the more they caught each other's eye. Two
30   boys approached the girls and asked them to dance. The girls stood
up and moved on to the floor with them. Furious at this betrayal, Mick
went for another drink to show her how unconcerned he was.

AT THE DISCO

When he got back the record had changed. He could not see the girl dancing; he could not see her friend either and he could not see them round the edge of the room. Someone else had taken their seats. They must have left with the two boys. They would be arm in arm walking down the street now. Or in a taxi. Close together on the back seat. Or in a shop doorway with their arms around each other. . . . Mick felt sick. The beer was always lousy in these places. He had another drink. It served him right. He should have made a move instead of standing there grinning like a fool. They would be making arrangements now to see each other tomorrow night. . . . And if that kid over there didn't stop staring at him, he was going to get a knuckle sandwich! . . . He felt tired. He had a headache. He would go and find Alan and tell him he was going home.

The girl came out of the Powder Room followed by her friend. For the benefit of foreigners and illiterates, there was a silhouette of a woman dressed in a crinoline on the door. The matching figure on the door of the men's lavatory wore top hat and tails.

Mick suddenly recovered. He had another drink. The beer had improved. His headache disappeared. He was no longer tired. Alan, who was still dancing with the blonde girl, caught his eye and leered at him from over her shoulder. His gloating attitude and apparent easy success, finally goaded Mick into action and he walked across to the girl in the blue dress and asked her if she would like to dance. The girl stopped talking to her friend and both girls stared at him. They appeared to be deciding by consensus. He was just getting ready to walk away, when the girl in the blue dress nodded briefly and walked past him on to the dance floor. Her manner was so aloof that she seemed to be leaving him rather than intending to dance.

The other girl smiled after her and tried to look unconcerned. But as soon as her friend had gone, she turned round and went into the Powder Room again.

The music was too loud to speak while they were dancing. The girl did not look as if she wanted to anyway. In spite of all the previous looks between them, she was behaving as if she had never seen Mick before. She contrived to look everywhere but into his eyes.

At the end of the record, she nodded a thank you and started to walk off the floor. Mick followed her, trying desperately to think of something to say before she reached her friend who, freshly brushed and perfumed, was waiting for her with a relieved smile. Just before she reached her, Mick said:

'Would you like a drink?'

The girl stopped and turned round.

'Yes. All right.'

The crowded dance floor gave Mick an excuse to touch her as he guided her towards the bar. He could feel her hip moving underneath her dress and he was close enough to smell the perfume in her hair. In the dim light, her drop-earrings looked as black as jet, but every time
80 they caught a reflection from the glass globe revolving on the ceiling, they sparked to emerald green.

'What would you like to drink?'

Mick reached into his jacket pocket and looked at the coins in his hand. This was all he had left from the five pounds that he had
85 borrowed from his dad. The girl played with the gold locket round her neck while she decided. She seemed to be considering the spirit bottles clamped upside down in front of the mirror at the back of the bar. Mick checked his money again. The silver was outnumbered by the brown.

90 'I'll have a Coke, please?'

'Are you sure?'

It was a brave bluff in the circumstances.

'Yes, thank you. I'm just thirsty, that's all.'

Mick relaxed.
95 'With ice?'

They found seats under the fronds of a plastic palm tree in one corner. The room had been designed with a tropical theme. The tables and chairs were made of bamboo. Imitation creepers festooned the ceiling and a jungle had been painted on the walls.

100 There were so many dirty glasses on the table that they had to clear a space before they could put down their own drinks. The girl took a tissue out of her handbag and dabbed the table dry.

Mick said, 'They hadn't got any ice left.'

She picked up the warm glass. 'I'm not surprised, they never
105 have.'

She had a long drink, then put the glass down. The portion of the table that she had wiped was mottled with damp spots.

'I don't think I've seen you here before, have I?'

Mick had a sip of lemonade. It was the cheapest drink he could
110 buy.

'No, it's the first time I've been. My mate's just joined the army and we're having a night out before he goes away.'

'Have you been to that new place, Tramps?'

'Been? I shall soon be one if things don't improve.'
115 'What do you mean?'

'I'm on the dole. I can hardly afford to go anywhere.'

'Susan my friend is. Her standing over there, look.'

She pointed through an archway to her friend, who was talking

AT THE DISCO

to a boy on the edge of the dance floor. They were in silhouette like
120   the figures on the lavatory doors.

     'She's just come back from Blackpool. She had a job in a hotel
but she got the sack.'

     'What for?'

     'I'm not sure. She said the manager didn't like her, but I think it's
125   because she was always having boys in her room.' She began to grin.
'She told her mother she was homesick when she got back.'

     Susan and the boy began to dance. Mick said:

     'Have you got a job?'

     'I work at Brompton and Moore's.'

130   'What, the shoe shop?'

     'That's right.'

     Mick had another sip of lemonade. He was drinking it like a
short.

     'What's your name?'

135   The girl hesitated and adjusted one of the rings on her hand.

     'Karen, what's yours?'

     'Mick'

     'My auntie's got a dog called Mick. It's ever so fierce. It lets you
into the house, but when you want to go home, it stands in front of the
140   door growling and won't let you out.'

     In the main room, the disc jockey was screaming into the
microphone as if the building was on fire and there was no possible
means of escape . . . 'BRANEWSOUNSFROMPLAYBOYS! THELATESAN-
GREATESINLIVENERTAINMENATADAMNEVES!'

145   'Never heard of them,' Mick said.

     The disc jockey put on another record but continued to babble
on, and his inane chatter, combined with the incomprehensible lyrics,
produced a triumph of disharmony.

     Karen finished her drink and stood up.

150   'I like this. Do you want to dance?'

     Mick followed her out of the bar. With three pence left in his
pocket and drinking lemonade, he would have danced a polka with
her.

     Karen looked at him now and they smiled every time their eyes
155   met. They still did not touch each other, but they were partners now
and not just two people dancing face to face.

Understanding

1 At the beginning of this piece Mick watches the two groups of dancers very closely. One group is described in lines 0–13, the other, between lines 14–17. In your own words, how would you describe the differences between these two groups?

2 First impressions are often important. After reading lines 18–32 what, in your opinion, were Mick's first impressions of the 'girl in the blue dress'?

3 Why did Mick feel like 'going home' in line 45?

4 Line 57 has the two girls appearing to decide 'by consensus'. Look up the word 'consensus' in a dictionary and then explain why you think the writer used this word here.

5 'It was a brave bluff in the circumstances' (line 92). What do you understand this phrase to mean? What was the bluff? Why was it brave? What was so special about these circumstances?

6 Either:
(a) Suppose that after the second dance Karen goes to the cloakroom where she meets her friend Susan. Karen obviously wants to talk about Mick. What would she say to her friend? Write down the conversation they might have.
Or:
(b) It is now Mick's turn to visit the toilet and he, similarly, meets up with his friend Alan. Write down the conversation they might have as Mick attempts to describe his feelings for Karen.

Response

1 Discos and parties are obvious places for meeting new friends. Describe just such a first meeting, but try to capture some of the nervousness and uncertainty of the moment as well as its excitement.

2 Bluffing is sometimes the only way out of certain tight spots. Write about a time when a bit of bluffing was needed to get you out of trouble.

FIRST DATE

by David Williams

Alan: [*To the listener*] I'm not a shy person really, not as a rule, but it took me ages before I plucked up the courage to ask Janice out. Well, I mean, you feel stupid, don't you? You don't know what to say when you're not used to it. I suppose I'd never fancied anybody enough . . . or just been too busy playing football to think about it. I'm not like some blokes who'll go out with any bit of skirt just so's they can show off in front of their mates.

Janice, though . . . you won't find her in that crowd. I knew as soon as I saw her that she had a bit of, you know, class. I think that's what made me notice her the first time, waiting for the bus. It was the way she stood, the way she held her head as she looked about. Not snooty or anything, just . . . I don't know . . . right, natural. I remember we'd been playing away at Whitley, won and all, and I was just getting back on to the coach with Baz when I saw her. . . .

1 Inside the coach

Besides the noise of the coach engine idling, there is much chatter and laughter from the boys in the coach.

Alan: Hey, Baz, look at that girl over there.

Baz: What girl? There's a dozen of them, man.

Alan: The good-looking one, the blonde, over by the bus-stop.

Baz: Oh yeah. What about her? Do you know her or summat?

Alan: No, I've never seen her before. She's all right though, isn't she?

Baz: Yeah, she's all right. Why, do you fancy her? Hey, fellers, Boy Wonder's got his eyes on a tart! He's in love!

Boys: [*Laughter and jeers*]

Duggan: Who's the lucky girl, Alan?

Baz: It's that blonde lass over there, by the bus-stop.

Alan: Shut up, Baz, will you?

Duggan: Hey, I know her. Her name's Janice. Her dad's got that sweet-shop on Plessey Road. Mackenzie's. I've seen her in there weekends. Do you want me to chat her up for you, Alan? She might have a friend. I could show you how to go on.

Boys: [*Laughter*]

Alan: Get lost, Duggan. I don't need your help.

Duggan: [*Teasing* **Alan**] 'Oh darling, I cannot keep my secret from you any longer. All these years you've served me my dolly mixtures and never have you guessed my secret passion. I am fascinated by your cherry lips, your bulls' eyes. . . .'

Boys: [*Laughter*]

Alan: All right, Duggan, that's enough.

Duggan: What's the matter, mate? Can't you take a joke? Here, have a fag.

Alan: No thanks, I don't smoke.

Duggan: Oh sorry, I forgot. The big football star doesn't smoke. They're bad for your health. Not as bad as she'll be, mate. She'll rot your teeth.

Boys: [*Laughter*]

Baz: Give her a wave as we go by, lads. Big smiles!

Boys: [*More laughter and cheering as the coach drives off. The sound effects fade away*]

Alan: [*As narrator*] Yeah, that was a great start. A bunch of grinning apes on the coach gawping at Janice, and me in the middle doing a brilliant impression of a beetroot. She blushed too, though, I noticed that.

Well, anyway I knew now who she was and where she lived. All I had to do was go over there and ask her out. Oh, easy said! Tell you the truth though, I was a bit scared. You know what I did? Next Sunday afternoon I took the bus down Plessey Road, got off at the stop past Mackenzie's, then caught the next bus

FIRST DATE

back. Oh, she was in there all right. I could see her head through the window as I passed but, well, I was too scared to go in. Go in! I was even too scared to stand on the pavement outside!

All the next week I was thinking what to do, what to say when I went in there. When Sunday came I forced myself to walk down the street, open that sweet-shop door. . . .

2 Inside the Shop

A shop doorbell rings.

Janice: Yes, can I help you?

Alan: Er . . . yes . . . do you have chocolates?

Janice: Well, yes, what sort of chocolates do you want?

Alan: Pardon?

Janice: What sort would you like? Chocolates.

Alan: Oh, yes. Sorry. Those ones, please. Er, do you like those ones?

Janice: Pardon?

Alan: Those are the ones I like. Do you like those ones?

Janice: Very much.

Alan: I'll have those ones, then. Er, a half-pound box.

Janice: OK. Anything else?

Alan: No thank you. I mean . . . er . . . yes . . . sort of. Your name's Janice, isn't it?

Janice: That's right. How do you know that?

Alan: Somebody told me. Er . . . my name's Alan.

Janice: Hello, Alan. Do I know you?

Alan: No.

Janice: Oh.

Alan: Well, you might have seen me on a coach once. I play football for Newminster High. We played your school two weeks ago. We won four-two . . . you didn't see the game at all, I suppose?

Janice: I'm afraid I must have missed it.

Alan: Well. . . . I'll be off, then.

Janice: Yes. Nice meeting you.

Alan: Right. See you. Oh, er, by the way, you wouldn't fancy going to see a film on Saturday, at all? With me, I mean.

Janice: Well, I'm not sure. What's on?

Alan: Er, I don't know really. I've heard it's good though. I wondered if you would like to see it. With me, you know.

Janice:	All right, then. I live at the back of the shop. Would you collect me here at about seven?
Alan:	Right! Great! Well . . . see you Saturday, then.
Janice:	Fine.

[*The shop doorbell rings as* **Alan** *opens the door*]

Janice:	Oh, Alan!
Alan:	Yes?
Janice:	Could I have sixty-eight pence for the chocolates, please?
Alan:	Oh. Oh, yeah, sorry. [*Money chinks on the counter*] Right.
Janice:	Ta.
Alan:	See you Saturday, then.
Janice:	OK. Bye. [*The shop doorbell rings again as* **Alan** *goes out*]
Alan:	[*As narrator*] And that was it!

Funny thing, though. After a bit I began to wish I hadn't asked her out at all. I mean, I hadn't changed my mind about her – don't get me wrong. It was just that . . . I don't know, I started to get anxious, worried in case Saturday would turn out to be a right flop. I couldn't think what to wear. Surely she wouldn't expect me to wear a suit or anything? No, I'd just wear my normal gear, only smarten myself up a bit — yeah, wash my hair straight after I come in from the match, give it plenty of time to dry before seven. It was seven, wasn't it? Or did she say half-past seven? No, no, seven . . . I think.

3 Inside the shop

The shop bell rings.

Janice:	Hello, you're a good timekeeper.
Alan:	Yeah, well my mum bought me this watch for Christmas. Keeps me right, you know.
Janice:	Really?
Alan:	Yeah. Only I didn't want to be late, you know. First date and that.
Janice:	Yes, it is, isn't it?
Alan:	What?
Janice:	Your first date.
Alan:	Well, I've known a few . . . er . . . how do you know that?
Janice:	Just guessed. Have you been washing your hair?

43

FIRST DATE

Alan: Mm?

Janice: We'd better go. There's a bus at ten past seven, goes right past the Regal.

Alan: OK.

4 In the street

We hear the noise of traffic outside the cinema.

Alan: Here we are then. Let's see what's on. Oh. 'Curse of the Vampires. . . .'

Janice: No, that's next week. Here's this week's. [*Laughs*] I've seen this one, Alan. Have you?

Alan: What is it? 'Snow White and the Seven Dwarfs'! We can't go and see that!

Janice: Why not?

Alan: [*Groans*] I knew something like this would happen, I've felt it all day. Oh, and now it's starting to rain.

Janice: Don't let it get you down, Alan. I've got my brolly. Come on, there's a coffee bar just down the road. You can treat me if you like.
[*The traffic noise fades away*]

5 The coffee bar

Besides the sounds of the coffee bar, there is a jukebox in the background.

Alan: I've never been in here before.

Janice: It's not been open long.

Alan: Yeah, you can tell. It's not like that scruffy place round the corner from our school. Same old crowd, always round there lunchtimes. You ever been to our school?

Janice: Funny you should ask that. I was there this morning.

Alan: This morning!

Janice: Yes. I had an idea there might be a football match on. So I came down to see you.

Alan: You came down to watch the match! I didn't see you.

Janice: No, you were too involved in the game. Anyway, I kept out of the way. I didn't know whether you'd want me there. I didn't want to embarrass you in front of your friends.

Alan: Oh, you don't have to worry about them. I don't.

Duggan: [*Approaching*] Hello, hello, hello. What have we here?

Alan: Duggan! What are you doing here?

Duggan: It's a free country, mate. I've got as much right to drink coffee as you have. I'm with the lads. Hey boys, Roy of the Rovers is here, with 'friend'!

44

Boys:	[*Mixture of cheerful greetings and jeers*]
Duggan:	Mind, you're a sly one, aren't you? It's Janice, isn't it? You'll have to watch this one, Janice. You know what they say, the quiet ones are the worst.
Alan:	Look, Duggan, why don't you. . . .
Duggan:	See, he's blushing now, but he's a demon with the women, Janice.
Baz:	Come on, Duggan. Leave them alone now.
Duggan:	Shut up, will you? I'm having a conversation here. Anyway, mate, you've let me down. I thought you were going to ask her if she had a friend.
Janice:	What's wrong? Can't you find one for yourself?
Duggan:	What?
Janice:	Or are you scared of girls? Perhaps you need someone to show you how to behave.
Duggan:	All right, Lady Muck, I can take the hint. Let's go, lads. See if we can find some skirt.
Baz:	Good idea.
Duggan:	I don't think much of yours, Alan.
Alan:	The cheeky beggar. I'll. . . .
Janice:	Leave him, Alan. He's not worth it.
Alan:	No. Anyway you took pretty good care of him yourself.
Janice:	His sort are all the same. Full of talk, and scared of girls.
Alan:	I haven't got any room to talk. It took me all my time to ask you out.
Janice:	I was glad you were nervous. You might not believe this, Alan, but this is my first date too.
Alan:	Oh never!
Janice:	Don't be shocked. I don't go out with boys for the sake of it. I've been asked a few times but, well, I've never felt like going out with anyone. Until tonight.
Alan:	But. . . .
Janice:	I don't know, there was something about you that was right. You made me feel cheerful. I liked that.
Alan:	How do you feel now?
Janice:	Funny, it seems natural to be sitting here, somehow, as if we'd known each other for years.
Alan:	Yeah, I know what you mean. I feel like that now, too. What would you say now to a nice, quiet walk through town? Look, it's stopped raining.
Janice:	I would say that's a lovely idea. We could look in a few shop windows.
Alan:	Come on, then. And later on we'll call in at the chippie

FIRST DATE

for a slap-up meal, to celebrate.

Janice: OK. But what are we celebrating?

Alan: Our first date!

[*The coffee bar noise fades away*]

Alan: [*As narrator*] And that's how it was. No exotic meal by candlelight, with a gipsy fiddler floating between tables, just a steamy chippie with a bottle of sauce between us. I thought the whole evening went great, looking back. One thing I forgot, though, that was to give Janice the box of chocolates she sold me the day I asked her out. I found them still in my coat pocket after I'd kissed her goodnight and was on my way home. Still, they'll keep, won't they? I'll give them to her next time, eh?

Understanding

1   How would you describe the other boys' attitude and behaviour towards Alan in scene one? How old would you say they were? Why do you think Duggan in particular behaves in the way he does?

2   In scene two, how much evidence is there which suggests that Alan is unsure of himself as he speaks to Janice? List as many points as you can find, giving the reasons for your choice.

3   In scene three, why do you think that Janice suggested, rightly as it turned out, that this was Alan's first date? What clues must she have spotted?

4   During the opening lines of scene five (until Duggan approaches), Janice mentions to Alan that she had been at his school that morning to watch the match. Read these lines again carefully. What do they tell you about the type of girl Janice is? Give reasons for your answer.

5   Later in scene five another side of Janice seems to emerge. How would you describe the way she handles Duggan? What are your views on her remark that 'His sort (Duggan) are all the same. Full of talk, and scared of girls.'?

6   Either:
    (a) At the end of scene five Alan (as narrator) makes plain his reaction to the evening's events. Rewrite this final section, but this time with Janice as the narrator. What would her views be?
    Or:
    (b) 'First Date' was originally written as a play for the radio. In what ways does this come across to a reader or, more accurately, a listener? List as many points as you can find which demonstrate that the play is meant to be heard rather than seen.

Response

1   Explore the differences between a radio script and a television screenplay a little more. Write out a short radio script of your own which deals with some of the difficulties and tensions surrounding 'first dates'. Then attempt its transformation into a television play. What changes would need to be made as you concentrate more on what an audience would be seeing rather than on what they would be hearing?

To help you get started, here is one way of beginning a scene for television:

Inside the works' bus

Jenny is sitting in the bus. It is going-home time. Just as it is about to leave, a man rushes on and sits next to her.
It is *Ed.* In his haste, he has not realized who he has sat next to, almost squashing her.

Ed: Oh, God, not again! (*Mumbling, as he shifts to his end of the seat*) I'm sorry! Wasn't looking! Didn't mean it!
Jenny: (*Cool*) I'm all right. Don't upset yourself. (*Turns her head and looks out of her window*)
                    . . . now over to you.

manwatching
by Georgia Garrett

From across the party I watch you,
Watching her.
Do my possessive eyes
Imagine your silent messages?
I think not.
She looks across at you
And telegraphs her flirtatious reply.
I have come to recognize this code,
You are on intimate terms with this pretty stranger,
And there is nothing I can do,
My face is calm, expressionless,
But my eyes burn into your back.
While my insides shout with rage.
She weaves her way towards you,
Turning on a bewitching smile.
I can't see your face, but you are mesmerised I expect.
I can predict you: I know this scene so well,
Some acquaintance grabs your arm,
You turn and meet my accusing stare head on,
Her eyes follow yours, meet mine,
And then slide away, she understands,
She's not interested enough to compete.
It's over now.
She fades away, you drift towards me,
'I'm bored' you say, without a trace of guilt,
So we go.
Passing the girl in the hall.
'Bye' I say frostily,
I suppose
You winked.

Understanding and Response

1   Read the poem carefully several times. Now attempt to
     recreate the same scene from the two other points of view.
     Firstly re-tell it through the eyes of the boy, then take up the
     point of view of the other girl. Keep to the style of the original
     poem if it helps, and see how sharply you can draw the lines
     of divide and suspicion.

After a Quarrel

by John Richmond

Now one dilemma faced them both;
Into one another's brain.
Get in the warm again, but not do it first.
He stood a hundred yards away, and watched her back.
How to step across the concrete, forgive, be forgiven,
She sat on a bench in the freezing night, in the rain.
They had cursed, driven the last oaths in the language

Understanding and Response

1   Read through this 'jumbled' poem carefully. Remember that it is called 'After a Quarrel'. Now rearrange the seven lines in a way which makes most sense to you.

2   Compare your version with the original which you can find on page 160. Comment on both the similarities and dissimilarities of the two.

3   Now attempt the next move. If it helps you could call your follow on version 'Stepping Across the Concrete'. How could you best continue this incident in six or seven lines of similar poetry?

'Listen to GRAN'

by Robert Leeson

Warby was an overspill area, a moor village with an old ruined mill, a battered chapel and a great circle of council houses, raw and orange-grey, to the horizon. Gran had never liked it, missing her old gossips from the town, but Granddad had a big garden and pottered
5   to his heart's content, growing champion leeks and great crinkly winter cabbage.

Everything seemed the same as they drew up and the old couple came to the gate, meeting Kev with open arms as he tumbled like a plump puppy out of the car. They showed no surprise that Mum was
10   not with them. What had Dad told them? Jan wondered, and the thought struck her like a dart – when had he realized, how long ago had he secretly made up his mind about why Mum had gone? Then she pushed the thought away into that shadowed place at the back of her mind.

15   'Come on in, dinner's almost ready. Jan, love, you're looking peaky.'

'She's not eating enough. She wants her ribs lining.'

There was a great hug from Granddad that left her breathless, a quick peck from Gran and then they were in the cluttered front room
20   with its slippery leather settee and its faint smell of mothballs.

'I'll take our Geoff down to the Weavers,' said Granddad.

'All right, but it's on the table at one o'clock sharp.'

Dad and Granddad went out.

'Can I see the whippets, Granddad?'

25 'Ah, off you go, but don't stick your fingers in the wire, lad. They're not vegetarians.'

Now they were left alone, Gran and she.

'Come in the kitchen, Jan love. You can peel the apples for me.'

The kitchen window looked out on the moors and Jan stood by
30 the sink, taking in the view. She knew just then, with the new understanding she had gained this very day, why she hated the street and the narrow house Mum and Dad had bought. It had no horizon. No matter where you looked, brick and stone stood up to block out the view.

35 She felt Gran's brisk fingers tie an apron round her waist, and picked up the coring knife.

'I've a nice recipe for apple crumble you can have, Jan love. There's a good many have asked me for it, but I don't give it out to all comers. I had it from my Gran, what d'you think of that?'

40 Jan heard Gran's voice, but only later that day, in the car going home, did she take in the words. Gran rattled on:

'Some folk are all for doing their shopping in one grand slam. Get the car out, off to the supermarket, come home weighed down like a packhorse. I always say, buy a bit every day, buy fresh, keep
45 busy. I reckon they stick a penny or tuppence on everything at weekends.

'Hey, love, go easy on that knife. We shall have all core and no apple.'

'Sorry, Gran.'

50 'You've got good, strong fingers, and light, too. You should make good pastry. Course, you young women buy it all ready-made these days, don't you?'

Granddad and Dad passed by the kitchen window and Kevin came running in from the garden. Jan felt a pain in her chest. She had
55 been holding her breath while Gran talked.

No one spoke over dinner. That was the unwritten law in Gran's house. But, over the apple crumble, Granddad, fiddling with his belt, to let out a notch, grinned at Jan.

'Well, Jan, how's the study going? Bi-ology is it, eh, and
60 geography. And is it "O" or "A" levels, I always get those letters mixed up.'

' "O" level this summer, Granddad, the first exam's in a month's time. "A" levels come in two years' time.'

'Of course,' put in Gran, 'she could leave school this summer if

51

65   she wanted. She's well gone sixteen.'

      'Eh, what?' said the old man. 'Our Jan? No, she's a great scholar, she is. She could be a teacher, she could.'

      'Those houses cost a lot, you know, with that mortgage and all.' Gran was glaring at Granddad now.

70   'I don't know why they had to buy that place, any road,' said Granddad. 'They had a perfectly good council flat.'

      The two old people had forgotten their guests now.

      'Ah, but you don't get on in a council flat. Pay, pay, till they carry you out, like us.' Gran leaned her elbows on the table, a sure sign that

75   she was irritated. 'They can sell their place and get a new one, when our Geoff's finished his course. They'll need a place they can invite folks to. You can't have lecturers and managers and such people home to a council flat.'

      'What the 'ell does that matter, woman? Can't our lad get on in

80   the world without being posh, for God's sake?'

      'Kevin, love, you can get down,' snapped Gran.

      Eyes wide, Kevin slipped from his chair and ran out into the garden. Jan's father got up from his chair and shut the door.

      'Look, Mum, Dad, don't fall out over us. We're going to

85   manage. That course'll be finished in a year's time and then I'll get more than I ever did in production, and prospects. It's just going to be tight, that's all.'

      Gran turned and looked at Jan.

      'Our Jan'll help all she can, I'm sure. You have to do without

90   some things in this life.'

      She smiled, but there was an edge to her words.

      Granddad pushed back his chair.

      'Come on, Jan. I'll walk you up to Borley Top. Put some colour in those cheeks.'

95   'I was going to help Gran with the washing up.'

      'Give over, you can get enough of that at home. Come on lass, you take one dog, I'll take the other.'

      On the hillside beyond the houses, Granddad let the dogs go, tucked Jan's arm under his, and together they climbed slowly up the

100   slope. To the west the sky was awash with a gentle pink. To the east the grey was shading into a darker blue.

      'Hey up, lass. Soon be summer. We haven't seen you up here half enough this past winter. When your exams are over, you'll have to come up more. Don't wait for your Dad to bring you, he's got

105   enough on his plate. Bring Kev up on the bus.'

      'Thanks, Granddad.'

      At the top of the ridge, they looked down into distant hills and valley folds. Some were already hidden in mist. Jan realized that

Granddad was speaking to her.

110   'Jan, love. There'll be a reason for it. There will, you know. It won't be just like it seems.'

Jan choked.

'Don't, Granddad, please.'

'All right, chuck.' The old man slapped his hands against his
115 coat.

'Let's turn about then. It's a bit parky up here.'

He whistled up the dogs and they walked back without saying a word. But as they were about to leave the hill and walk down the estate track, the old man suddenly said fiercely:
120   'There's two words I can't abide and never could and I've heard 'em all my life. That's "do without". Why should we? Who says we should?'

The other three were waiting as they came up to the house, Dad and Kevin in coats and scarves. Gran kissed Jan lightly on her cheek
125 and slipped something into her pocket.

'Look after yourself, our Jan.'

Kev tugged at Jan's sleeve.

'Can I sit in the back with you, Jan?'

He scrambled on to the seat and arranged himself cat-like with
130 his head against her. Before the car had gone half a mile down the moor road, he had dozed off. Jan felt in her pocket. There were three pieces of paper, folded together, two pound notes and the recipe for apple crumble. She gazed out of the car window at the falling darkness. What was going to happen to them? What was going to
135 happen to her?

Gran was quite sure. Jan was going to take her mother's place, look after Dad and Kev, because Mum wasn't coming back. Granddad was sure things weren't what they seemed.

Who could she believe? Who was this woman they called Mum,
140 all these years? And where, where was Mum?

Understanding

1   At the beginning of this extract the village of Warby is briefly described. What impressions do you have of the place from those first few lines? Give reasons for your answer.

2   Look carefully at the way Kev, Jan and her dad are greeted by the grandparents (lines 7–28). What does this opening section tell you about the 'old couple'? Had they been discussing things between themselves? Why do you think

'listen to GRAN'

this? In what ways do the grandparents differ in their
approaches to Jan and her family?

3   Gran and Jan were alone as they talked in the kitchen (lines
28–52). What evidence is there to suggest that Jan was not
very relaxed or involved in this conversation? Why do you
think she behaves in the way she does?

4   Between lines 56 and 80, there are several occasions when
Granddad openly disagrees with Gran. Using your own
words, briefly describe these disagreements.

5   Re-read from line 82 to the end of the extract. From all that
you have now read, try putting yourself in Jan's place. How
would you answer Jan's three questions? Who should she
believe — Gran or Granddad? What sort of woman was
'Mum'? Why might she have left home?

6   Either:
(a) Write down the conversation that Jan would have had
with her father as they drove home from Warby.
Or:
(b) After Jan and her family have left, Gran and Granddad
talk about their visit and the problems they face. What
would their conversation be?

Response

1   Having to cope with new and unexpected responsibilities
can be very difficult for all concerned. Write about a time
when you have had to adapt and change your way of life
because of totally unforeseen events.

2   'Grandparents always know best.' Is this always true? Write
about a time when you have strongly disagreed with the
opinions or advice being offered by an older or wiser person.

13

Gregory's girl
—the cookery class

by Bill Forsyth, Andrew Bethell and Gerald Cole

SCENE 6		**The cookery class**
		(Carol, Liz, Susan, Ann and others set up the Home Economics room. They are making pastry.)
	CAROL	Did you hear about the trial?
5	**LIZ**	Trial?
	CAROL	Football trial. Dorothy joined it.
	LIZ	And about time too.
	SUSAN	Why is it boys are such a physical disaster?
	CAROL	Apparently Phil wouldn't let her play.
10	**SUSAN**	Too much to lose I expect.
	CAROL	Well, she stuck it out and showed him up something rotten.
	ANN	Oh God, not pastry. I hate pastry and it hates me. Give me a goulash anyday. It doesn't fight back.
15	**CAROL**	She scored three times with him in goal.
	SUSAN	Poor Phil.
	LIZ	Have you seen his moustache?
	CAROL	Anyway he's got to pick her now.
	LIZ	Men's hair fascinates me. It's so temporary.
20	**ANN**	Equal parts of Trex and lard. Isn't that it?
		*(The boys are coming in for the lesson. It is a mixed lesson. **Steve** is in first. He is a professional. Already he has his bench organised.)*
	STEVE	Anyone seen Gregory? He's meant to be working
25		with me . . . oh dear Lizzie, not the hands. Lay off the hands till the last possible minute.

(*Gregory is late and makes his way through the girls. He is trying to be both charming and surreptitious.*)

30 **GREGORY** Sorry I'm late.
    STEVE Where've you been?
    GREGORY Football.
    STEVE Playing?
    GREGORY No . . . watching. From afar.
35 **STEVE** Hands!

(*Gregory shows him his hands. It is a routine inspection.*)

    GREGORY That's just paint there.
    STEVE I've got the biscuit mix started, you get on with the
40 sponge and put the oven on, four hundred and fifty degrees.
    GREGORY Yes, boss.

(*Susan aproaches Steve. She is wearing a worried look and a grotty apron.*)

45 **SUSAN** Steve, can you help me out with this pastry mix thing?
    GREGORY Hello, Susan.

(*Gregory is ignored.*)

    STEVE Pastry? What pastry? There's more than one kind
50 you know. Is it rough puff, short crust . . . flaky . . . suet . . . ?

(*Susan's face is a blank.*)

    Just tell me, what are you making?
    SUSAN A meat pie. Margaret's doing the Strudel Soup, and
55 I'm doing the pie. It's the eggs for the pastry that I'm not sure of . . .
    STEVE Strudel Soup, eh? I'd like to try some of that. It's
NOODLE soup, and what eggs? You don't put eggs in a pastry. It's 8 ounces flour, 4 ounces
60 margarine . . .
    GREGORY . . . a pinch of salt . . .
    STEVE . . . some salt, mix it up, into the oven, fifteen minutes . . . and that's it, okay? No eggs, no strudels, nothing.
65 **SUSAN** Is that all? That's *simple*, really easy. (*She wanders off.*)

*   *   *

EXTRACT A

'Yes, boss,' Gregory turned enthusiastically to the work surface at his side. Steve — always liable to be touchy in these surroundings — was placated. Gregory could talk to him when the cake mix — or whatever it happened to be — was safely installed in the oven. He snapped open the cupboard doors below the worktop, reached out a large plastic mixing bowl and slapped it on the top, gently nudging Steve, who was already mixing at a speed to put most blenders to shame. 'Sorry,' said Gregory.

Steve, long inured to his partner's culinary ineptitude, nodded slowly. As if to cement his position of supremacy, a pretty girl with straight shiny dark hair chose that moment to appear at his side.

'Steve,' she said, 'can you help me out with this pastry mix thing?' Her apron was awry and she looked confused.

'Hello Susan,' said Gregory, rising.

She gave him a cool glance and turned her attention to Steve, who sighed theatrically and laid down his whisk.

He turned to her slowly, the prophet descending from the mountain. It was plainly a role he enjoyed. 'What kind of pastry? There's more than one, you know. Is it rough puff, short crust, flaky, suet . . . ?'

A horrified blankness overtook Susan's face.

Steve took pity. 'Just tell me, what are you making?'

Susan sighed. 'A meat pie. Margaret's doing the strudel soup, and I'm doing the pie. It's the eggs for the pastry I'm not sure about . . .'

This was too much for Steve to resist. A broad smile split his face. 'Strudel soup eh? I'd like to try some of that.' He glanced at the still hovering Gregory, who smiled thinly; he had no idea what Steve was on about but instinctively he had no wish to upset Susan.

'It's *noodle* soup,' Steve declared. 'And what eggs? You don't put eggs in a pastry. It's eight ounces of flour, four ounces of margarine . . .'

'. . . A pinch of salt,' Gregory threw in helpfully.

'. . . Some salt,' Steve continued. 'Mix it all up, into the oven for fifteen minutes, and that's it. OK? No eggs, no strudels, nothing.'

His sarcasm evidently had greater effect on Susan than the advice.

'Is *that* all?' she said, tossing her head. 'That's *simple.*'

Gregory's girl
—the cookery class

	STEVE	To think there are five guys in fifth year crying themselves to sleep over that.
	GREGORY	Six, if you count the music teacher.
70	**STEVE**	Watch your mixing, it goes stiff if you overdo it, thirty seconds is enough. Give me the sugar.
	GREGORY	It's time *you* were in love. Take your mind off all this for a while . . .
	STEVE	Plenty of time for love. I'm going to be a sex
75		maniac first. Start this summer. Get rid of my apron and let my hair down, put love potions in my biscuits. Anyway I want to be rich first, so that I can love something really . . . expensive.
	GREGORY	You're daft. You should try it. Love's great.
80	**STEVE**	Who told you?
	GREGORY	I'm in love. *(He means it. He is abstractedly stirring the sponge mix with his finger.)* I can't eat, I'm awake half the night, when I think about it I feel dizzy. I'm restless . . . it's wonderful.
85	**STEVE**	That sounds more like indigestion.
	GREGORY	I'm serious.
	STEVE	Or maybe you're pregnant, science is making such progress . . . (*Steve extracts Gregory's finger from the mixing bowl and starts to wipe it*
90		*clean.*) Come on, who is it? Is it a mature woman? Did you do anything dirty? Did you wash your hands?
	GREGORY	Don't be crude.
	STEVE	Come on! Who is it?
95	**GREGORY**	You'll just laugh, and tell people.
	STEVE	Give us a clue.
	GREGORY	(*Reluctantly*) It's somebody in the football team.
	STEVE	(*Silent for a moment*) Hey, that's really
100		something. Have you mentioned this to anyone else? Listen, it's probably just a phase . . . is it Andy, no, no . . . is it Pete?

EXTRACT B

Gregory stared at him, appalled. 'Come on! I mean Dorothy. She came into the team a couple of days ago. She's in 4A.' Sweet memory melted his outrage. 'She's a wonderful player. She goes round with Carol and Susan. She's got lovely long hair, she always looks really clean and fresh and she smells, mmm . . .' He was grinning now with a kind of helpless idiocy. 'Gorgeous . . . Even if you just pass her in the corridor. And she's got teeth, lovely teeth, lovely white, white teeth . . .'

'Oh *that* Dorothy,' said Steve. 'The hair . . . the smell . . . the teeth. *That* Dorothy.'

With the prospect of startling revelations receding, Steve's interest waned; he went back to his rolling pin.

'That's her, that's Dorothy,' Gregory leaned forward excitedly, planting one hand on the work top, missing it and landing in his mixing bowl instead.

'The one that took your place in the team,' said Steve dourly.

'So what? She's a good footballer.' Gregory considered the remark almost rude; he began to scrape sponge mix off his hand. 'She might be a bit light but she's got skill; she's a fantastic girl . . .'

'Can she cook?' said Steve. 'Can she do this?' He scooped a wafer thin disc of pastry off the worktop and juggled it in the air with a pizza-maker's flourish.

This struck Gregory as unnecessarily flippant. It was beginning to dawn on him that infatuation was likely to be a lonely business.

'When you're in love,' he declared solemnly, 'things like that don't matter.'

'Gimme the margarine,' said Steve.

An objective observer might have detected a hint of envy in his tone, but Gregory was too involved in his own state of mind; he needed reassurance. 'Do you think she'll love me back?' he asked tentatively. He handed over the margarine, picked up his fork and began stirring again.

'No chance,' said Steve. 'Watch that mix. I told you, nice and slowly. Take it easy . . .' He took Gregory's hands in his, guiding him through the motions of a correct mixing. Central as it was to Steve's preoccupations, it was still a friendly act. They were, after all, mates.

Gregory tried again. 'What do you mean, no chance?'

Steve sucked his teeth; he would go no further; prolonged discussion could ruin a good baking. 'No chance,' he said flatly.

Gregory looked glum. For the first time unease joined the rather pleasant nervous tingling he felt and he wasn't at all sure if he liked it. At least, he consoled himself, he'd made sure no one else was aware of his predicament.

Understanding

1   Steve is the first boy to arrive for the cookery lesson. He is described in the playscript as 'a professional'. What do you think is meant by the word 'professional' here? Is there any evidence which supports this description of him?

2   Compare lines 42–66 from the playscript, with Extract A (from the novel version of *Gregory's Girl*). It is the same scene but several differences should be clear. For example, what 'extra' do you learn about the three main characters from the novel version of the play? Which type of lines have been left out of the play version? Why do you think these particular lines were omitted?

3   Re-read lines 72–86. What are your impressions of Gregory from these brief comments? What kind of boy is he?

4   From line 102 until the end of the scene, the relevant section from the novel version has been substituted for the remaining playscript. From what you know so far, and using the novel version as a guide, complete the remaining playscript yourself. What will you keep? What will you omit? What, if anything, will you change?

5   Compare your playscript version with the original (which you can find on page 160). How similar are they? List the main differences between the two script versions. Which do you prefer and why?

Response

1   In *Gregory's Girl*, a girl beats the boys at football and a boy beats the girls at cookery. Think of other situations where traditional sex–role expectations might be disturbed or upset — fourth year girls working successfully in the Wood, Metal or CDT areas — a group of boys deliberately opting for a child-care course within 'Life Skills' or PSE. There must be many other possibilities in and out of classrooms, on and off the sports field.

   Place your incident in a setting you know well. Your own school may well be the best place. Then write a scene in play form, or as a short story, which really brings this clash of expectations out into the open. Remember, humour can often be an effective weapon if you want to make a serious point in an entertaining way.

14

AT THE HAIRDRESSERS

A fifth former's view of work experience. Extracts from a diary kept last winter by Karen Blakey, when she was a pupil at Biddick School, Washington, Tyne and Wear. She is now on a two-year, full time course in hairdressing and beauty at Newcastle College of Arts and Technology.

Hair!

Day one: 6.30am. Had a shower to wash the sleep out of my system. I was working in a hairdressing salon so the least I could do was wash my hair.

WASH THE SLEEP OUT.

I was very much looking forward to it. I felt nervous though. I imagined walking in the room and everyone looking but nobody speaking. Then everyone bursting out into fits of laughter at my obnoxious yellow apron with green spots. It was the only thing I could get my hands on.

The bus made its way slowly to Sunderland. We arrived there just after 9.00am. I was late. My first morning. What was Mrs Sinclair going to think.

I explained about how the roads were bad, and she was OK and quick to show me where to take off my wet things. I entered the staffroom expecting the chatter to stop and everyone to stare, but the voices went on and no one stared.

Mrs Sinclair showed us where everything was. All I could think of was the embarrassment if I did do something wrong. I was bound to forget some of the many things she was telling us.

Everyone seemed happy and friendly towards each other. I felt so out of place, like an immature kid. Coming in from school to this place, I would be doing basically the same kind of work as they were doing, only I wouldn't get paid for it. This was going to be a great experience for me though. Something that was going to tell me what I was going to do when I left school.

61

AT THE HAIRDRESSERS

The girl that was to show me the ropes was a junior called Danielle. I watched her as she cleaned the rollers with another girl, Katrina (I liked her hair). They weren't watching what they were doing. It was a habit. They knew exactly what to do. The drier and the washing machine were both humming behind me. Girls were in and out like robotic yo-yos.

The shop was empty. There was only one client in. She was getting a perm. I went over to watch.

Mrs Sinclair saw me watching and asked if I would like to hand the cement papers and curlers to Alwin, the girl who was doing the perm. I was pleased to and quickly picked up a curler and cement paper. Alwin speedily snatched them out of my hand. She talked all the time to the client asking her things about her family, her plans for holidays, just little things. She must have really made her feel like royalty.

When she had put the plastic bag over the curlers, I took the perm tray away and placed the curlers in their correct boxes, threw out the cotton wool and washed the rest of the dirty things.

My coffee break was for 15 minutes, but after 10 minutes I was cleaning up hair with a brush from underneath a chair; I just wanted to be busy all of the time. I scraped through my ideas to find something else to do. I ended up washing some cups out then folding more towels.

I spent most of the afternoon washing the used basins, folding towels and looking at the drifting snow out of the window. Talking to the customers was hard. I was very nervous but forced words out like 'Would you like a cup of coffee?' or, 'Would you like a magazine?' It was great. I was thoroughly enjoying myself, even though I wasn't doing much. All the time I was watching, listening and learning.

Many people had commented on my hair. They seemed to like it. I hoped they liked me.

Mrs Sinclair said it would be fine if I went early because of the low business. My first day was finished. It had been great. Wonderful. The staff were 'canny', the clients were interesting.

I was going to really enjoy this week. My feet were sore, I had hardly sat down all day . . . but I was looking forward to tomorrow.

Day Two: The morning was boring. All the towels were washed, dried, folded and put back on the shelves above the sinks, all the basins and measuring boxes were washed and as usual the work area was spotless.

A woman was in the shop getting a perm. I hurried over as the hairdresser began to perm the shampooed hair. Passing the rollers and papers I felt more useful.

The woman smiled and commented on how enthusiastic I looked, how patient I looked with such a boring job. But I wasn't bored. I knew I would be if I had to do it all the time, but it was better than just watching and more professional than folding the towels.

The afternoon was much better. There were plenty of dishes, a bin full of dirty washing, and dried, wrinkled towels ready for folding.

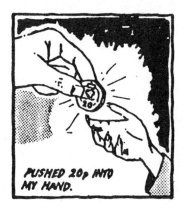

PUSHED 20p INTO MY HAND.

Brushing the floor, I noticed the woman from the morning. The hairdresser was drying her curly hair. I returned the brush to its box and went to watch her technique. This was the first client that I had really talked to without that uncomfortable feeling in the pit of my stomach. I laughed as she admired her hair in the mirror. She was really pleased. I told her it was lovely, which wasn't a lie.

When the hairdresser went to the cash desk to work out the bill the old lady took out her purse and pushed 20 pence into my hand. I could feel my cheeks burning with embarrassment but as I thanked her I felt so proud.

At 4.50pm I finished: the end of my second day. It was going so fast. I wished in a way I could leave school and just stay there. Forget my exams. But that was just fantasy.

Day Three: The bus was late and I arrived in the salon for 9.15am. Nobody said anything though. They joked on as I took of my ugly wellies and black leg warmers and I laughed, glad to be noticed.

Margaret asked me to take a woman out from under the hair drier and release her from the curlers that were embedded in her head. She was old and grey, but she had a nice happy face formed by wrinkles. I jumped at the chance.

Taking the net from off the curlers was embarrassing, it kept catching on the clips. My heart started thumping harder as I felt the rollers pulling, but it came off and I immediately begun unrolling the rollers. I couldn't help smiling to myself. I felt I was doing something that was more like the hairdressing profession. Instead of just passing curlers or watching, I was in contact with the client. I was part of a hair-do.

I was told that I was going to be 'promoted' to hair washing. My first

client was again grey haired with green eyeshadow.

I took her to the sink area, asked her to sit down, and put a towel round her shoulders. The water was set to the right temperature and I began to soak the hair with the adjustable shower. The hose disappeared down a small hole beside the tap and appeared again with a tug. Tugging too hard sent a stream of water running down the woman's face. Disaster had struck. My cheeks burned as I said 'Sorry'. She just laughed.

In the afternoon I washed five more clients' hair and even combed one woman's through. I was beginning to feel like a real hairdresser.

I was getting faster at everything by the end of the day. Uncurling, washing hair, washing dishes, folding towels, unloading and loading the washing machine and drier. I was getting more confident. Therefore I was getting bored with it. I didn't want to do anything hard, like perming and cutting. I just wanted to get more involved.

This week was definitely showing just how much I wanted to be a hairdresser. I had doubted it before. Just thought it might be wanting to do it because it seemed nice working with all those colours and making people happy with successful hair cuts. But this showed me

AT THE HAIRDRESSERS

that the beginning and even the end wasn't as glamorous as it looked, and I was still interested. I had found my future profession.

Day Four: By 11 o'clock I was bored, with an aching head through lack of sleep. There was nothing to do.

Alwin asked me, as I strutted slowly up and down the shop floor, to wash her client's hair. When that was done, though, it was back to the kitchen and on with filling the washer and emptying the drier: boring. I couldn't blame it on the girls. It was just that there wasn't much business.

Even though I was bored I still wanted so much to have a job there and be able to wear one of the orange overalls (even though they weren't really to my liking).

I passed the curlers to Pam as she was 'winding a perm'. How skilfully she worked with her hands. I wished I was in her place. What I would give if Mrs Sinclair asked me to stay on. I wondered if she had noticed how hardworking and dedicated I was.

At 12.45pm I was back washing neutralizing dishes and, again, folding towels.

I watched Judith blow-waving an old woman's hair. She had her eyes closed as the hot air blew over her face. Judith called me over.

'Would you let me cut your hair?' she said still making circular rotations with the brush through the thick grey hair. I was shocked. Feeling myself going red I smiled to hide the embarrassment. David had told me not to let anyone cut my hair. He was my usual hairdresser and I didn't want to upset him. I was in an awkward position. She could see how I felt.

'I wouldn't change the style or anything. Just make it better here and there.' She paused. 'Can I?'

Well, there was no real harm was there? I agreed. It would get me to know Judith better anyway; I hadn't really talked to her.

At last 4.45 came, and sure enough I was sitting in a chair putting a brush through my intensely lacquered hair. I felt embarrassed, and more of the staff gathered round and looked at the way my hair was cut. They laughed and joked on with me calling me 'madam' and things like that. I felt great. If only I had a week left, instead of a day.

Judith came and showed them the many mistakes David had made. I felt as if it was my fault, even though it wasn't. I listened to what she was saying, though, because she was talking sense.

She was really enjoying snipping away at my hair. She changed it a bit, but I must admit, it was for the better. I could go on for ages about the feelings and thoughts I was having. I felt absolutely wonderful. They were really talking to me and giving me a chance to answer back.

Day Five: I got on with work straight away. It was my last day and I was going to make sure I didn't waste a moment by dawdling around.

I felt sad as the day went on. I was talking to the staff much more and knew it was all going to stop. Back to school on Monday. Oh, how I wished I could work here. It would be great to get a Saturday job but plucking up the courage to ask Mrs Sinclair was the problem.

When I got back after dinner it was busy. The sink was full of dishes from both the salon and staff's dinners and we were running low on towels.

We had to put the towels straight into the drier without washing them first. It took about 30 minutes to clear the sink. I did it all by myself.

I didn't stop after that: even Mrs Sinclair was sweeping the floor. I went to the shop for Coffeemate, passed curlers, swept the floor, folded the towels, washed the dishes, made up perm trays, made coffee for clients and watched the

techniques the hairdressers used that afternoon. A really fast moving afternoon.

I was thinking of my small task with Mrs Sinclair.

She was working through some papers in her small office. I took a deep breath and popped my head round the corner.

'Mrs Sinclair', I started. 'Do you think there's any chance of a Saturday job here?' I could feel myself (as usual) going red with embarrassment.

'Well Karen', she said, 'I'd love to keep you on because I've been really pleased with the way you've worked. You've

worked really hard. But we've already got two girls when we should really only have one, but as soon as there is a place I'll let you know.' I was filled with hope and longing.

At five o'clock Mrs Sinclair told me I could go. I could have polished the benches away if it meant prolonging my stay.

I felt sad but happy. I had made lots of friends and I was a bit more sure of my future. As I walked out Mrs Sinclair said she hoped to see me again. Little did she know how much I was hoping for the same thing.

AT THE HAIRDRESSERS

Understanding

1   Reading through the entry for Day One, what is the first
     impression you have of the other girls working in the salon?
     Give examples to support your answer.

2   At one stage during Day One, Karen writes of a client being
     made to 'feel like royalty'. What exactly do you think she
     means by this phrase? Be as precise as you can.

3   Day Two has Karen receiving a 20p tip from a client, for
     which she felt 'so proud'. Why did she feel this? What was so
     special about this small act of generosity?

4   Day Three includes the accident with the shower hose. Read
     this section again and then re-write the incident from the
     point of view of the woman who was splashed. What might
     she be feeling and thinking as she watched young Karen at
     the sink?

5   Either:
     (a) Karen returns home after a day at the salon and starts to
     tell her mother about the day's events. Write down what she
     would say and how her mother might respond.
     Or:
     (b) No Saturday job was available for the moment. School
     started again on Monday. What would 'David' say when he
     discovers that Karen's hair had been cut? . . . Continue with
     Karen's diary for a day or so. How might things develop?

Response

1   Write about a work experience or Saturday job that you
     have been involved with. Pay particular attention to the way
     people behaved towards each other and how you felt about
     the whole experience.

2   Career decisions can often go wrong. Write about a time
     when a job someone had been looking forward to turned out
     to be much worse than had originally been expected.

15

Diary..... of a professional Footballer

by Eamon Dunphy

28 September

We have Carlisle at the Den tomorrow. Another home win, and we will be really up there in the top five. And the best part of the season for us is yet to come. But there is a bad atmosphere, a lazy atmosphere, a kind of brooding greyness hanging over the place.

What we are doing is going to Crystal Palace on Mondays. We get changed, and finally start around 10.45. We have ten minutes running around doing exercises. Then we have twelve-a-side because the apprentices are there too. Two-touch football on a very narrow pitch. So everyone kicks the ball into each other's balls, and it is over the roof and all over the shop. I'm in goal one end, Gordon Bolland is in goal the other. So one whole morning — nothing. On Tuesday we go out and run our cobs off for half an hour, then we get the ball and play five-a-side. So again, nothing. Wednesday we have off. So there seems to be nobody really interested in correcting our basic faults, in working at the game.

The balance of the side is not right yet either. We have got a kid playing outside left who is not ready yet. Dennis is sitting on the bench tomorrow, which is ridiculous. He is one of our more positive players. It is obvious that without him we are not such a good side as we are with him. It is only a matter of time, until we lose a game, and then Benny will put him in. Then Benny will say 'Now we are back to our best. This is us.'

But I cannot understand why he does not do it now. Why do we have to lose before we pull ourselves together? Why not work and organize ourselves now?

29 September

Millwall 1   Carlisle United 2

'No way can we lose this game. Carlisle never beat us at home. Not many sides do, but certainly not the Carlisles of this world.' That was what we went out thinking. It was just a matter of waiting for the goal to come. We will get the first goal, and then start playing a bit, and the other one or two will come. We've done it a hundred times, we've done it two hundred times. Same old thing; dead easy.

They were desperate. They had lost at home, they had lost everywhere. They lost one game 6–0. So we started off. The pitch was bumpy, and it was very windy. In the first quarter of an hour we had one, maybe two, chances. Just little flurries, but nothing occurred. We were all kind of suspended in mid-air. No one was doing anything. But we were not worried. 'We will get a chance, and it will be in the back of the net.'

We did not respect them. A lot of them were just waiting for us to score. But there was one little guy in midfield who was working his heart out. Positive, making runs, tackling, jumping, getting involved. He seemed to be one of the few players on their side who wanted to play. I just looked at him and thought 'Ten out of ten for effort, but you are wasting your time.'

So half-time came and it was 0–0. We were kicking into our favourite end in the second half. We had got the wind as well. Everything was right. A couple more near misses. Alfie missed an absolute sitter. That should have been the first goal.

Sides do not lose at the Den; they commit suicide. They wait for you to score. They offer you the game on a plate. Carlisle had offered us the game on a plate, but we had not taken it.

Now there was uneasiness, the first hint of doubt; a bit of desperation crept in. Alfie's miss was crucial. You think 'That's ominous. We won't get an easier chance than that. This is not going to be the day.'

They began to see that there was nothing to be afraid of. They were beginning to play a little bit more. They were beginning to think they could win. And we were beginning to realize we could fail to win. And then we thought 'We will switch it on.' But we could not. It just got worse and worse. In the middle of the second half it just got unbelievable. Nobody could pass the ball, nobody could find it, nobody wanted the ball, nobody wanted to do anything at all positive. People were putting their heads on their chest, and looking around, blaming other people. And everybody was getting edgy.

Then, ten minutes from the end, Brownie — he is overweight and having a nightmare — *blasts* a ball back to Kingy. Kingy had no chance. It flew past him, hit the post, and came back into his arms. He turned round and lashed it upfield. One of their defenders headed it out, Gordon hit it first time, and it was in the back of the net.

I could not even raise my arms. I was embarrassed. We did not deserve it. I did not do a war dance. I just stood there and said 'Well, thank Christ for that! We have got away with it again.' Everyone was pleased now, it was a matter of holding out for eight or nine minutes. Well, we did not even think in terms of holding out. We thought 'That's it, it is over.' We knocked it about for five minutes. They had jacked it in, except for that last desperate spurt every away team makes.

Some guy hit an aimless ball into the box. Kitch — there was not an opponent near him — headed it back to Kingy. But Kingy had come out instead of staying on his line, hadn't given Kitch a call, and it was in the back of the net. It bounced twice, and we thought Kingy had it. Always gets those balls, he is good at it. But not this time. It was Kingy's fault basically. Because he did not shout. Again it is all part of this thing he has been going through. It's predictable. You knew it had to happen some time. But you never thought . . . And now it is 1–1. Christ! I held my head in my hands and thought 'This is unbelievable!'

And this paralysing feeling came over me. There was no answer to it. So anyway, we had dropped a point. We got a little desperate, but I knew we would not get it now. There was no real desire to win.

Now they were steaming, Carlisle. They could not believe it. Energy! Positive runs! They were calling for the ball; they were knocking it around; they were ten feet tall. Transformation. To come to Millwall and get a point!

So they boot a ball upfield, a fellow gets it, Kingy comes tearing out of his box, scythes the winger down. For no apparent reason. Free kick. Fellow takes it. The centre half has come up, heads it, it hits Kitch and then the back of the net. In the net!

I looked around again. I could not believe it. It really was like a bad dream. It is impossible to lose at home to Carlisle any time, but having been 1–0 up with ten mintues to go, it was unbelievable.

We went off and got in the bath. We had been diabolical. We had produced the kind of football that our training had threatened all season. Inept, grey, sterile, nothing football. No energy, nothing.

Diary..... of a professional Footballer

Nobody said anything. We just sat there, disbelief on everybody's face. Muttering about Kingy, muttering about this, muttering about that. And I was angry. I had not played well. I was annoyed at that. But I was not so much annoyed because we had not played well, but because the signs had been there for a good two weeks.

I don't like getting drunk, but tonight I feel 'I'm going to get drunk.' There is nothing else for it.

I have never felt ashamed about Millwall until today. I have felt proud about them always. The character, the skill, the results we have got away from home . . . you are proud to play for Millwall. You think 'What a good set of lads. What a good club to play for.' But this . . . it was such a waste. To get beaten like that!

30 September

So I came home last night and had a few drinks. But it doesn't help. When you wake up in the morning, you think 'It didn't happen' or you try to block it out. But it happened. And when you read the Sunday papers you soon learn that it did.

Sunday is very much a down day anyway. You build up all week emotionally and physically to Saturday. You get really wound up, then bang! Saturday afternoon it all comes out. Even the games that look diabolical to people watching, games where nothing has been achieved, nothing creative anyway, you come off the park thinking 'Gotta get in that bath. Jesus!' You have put everything into it physically and emotionally, oblivious of the fact that it is drivel. And by Sunday you are no good for anything.

When you've won, it isn't so bad. Alan and I both have this routine of getting the Sunday papers, looking at the League table, working out who is playing who next week, where it will leave us — 'five points behind, but if they lose it'll only be three', all that sort of thing. But when you've lost like we did yesterday, when even you are conscious you've been in a load of rubbish, the Sunday papers you do not need.

1 October

This morning everyone seemed to have forgotten last Saturday. We are at Sheffield on Wednesday, Forest on Saturday, and the feeling is 'Well, we'll try and nick something there.'

The lads are sick, I suppose, in their own way. But footballers are resilient. They bounce back quickly as a group. Jokes, birds, you talk about anything. Even football. Some of the lads do anyway. When you get older you start talking about the game a bit, seeing things you never saw before, feeling responsible for things you never felt responsible for before. It becomes more difficult to shrug things off.

So we started training. A bit of running to get warmed up, then we were going to have this practice match. Lawrie was handing the bibs out. And he walked past me. 'That is very odd of him.' I thought nothing of it; just a little bit perturbed. I looked after him, and he was giving out first-team shirts. And he was giving one to Robin Wainwright . . . and he gave one to Dennis . . . and I looked around . . . 'I'm dropped! No! But I am!'

I could not believe it. I could not think for a minute. And Benny was standing there as if nothing had happened. No one said anything to me.

He had given me a reserve shirt. 'Play in midfield,' he said. How do you react? It was like somebody had plunged a dagger in my back. I was so hurt. Not so much because I was dropped, but because they had done it like that.

And they could not do it to me! I was choked. I had been playing reasonably well; certainly better than a lot of other people. And I cared! I was part of it. This was me, this was the lads. And then BANG! I'm out of it.

So he said 'Let's have the first-team lads over here. You lot go and have a kick about at the far end.' So they had all gone away, the lads, for a team talk. And I went up the other end with the youngsters. I could not believe it.

I could feel tears welling up in my eyes, but I thought 'Nah, that's no good.' So I just stood there for about five or ten minutes. I don't know how long it was. I can't remember how long the talk went on. The young lads were knocking it about, and I looked round, and there was this little group, and Benny was talking to them. And you feel so left out.

And there's the hurt. It just happens. A snap of the fingers, and you are gone. Out. All the commitment, all the emotion, all the hard work, all the belief. Everything gone. Because some idiot fooled around at the back in the last eight minutes on Saturday.

And my first reaction then was to walk out. There and then. But I thought 'No, anybody can be dropped. Now you have got to show you are a man. Now you have got to show you are big.'

So I made a few jokes with the young lads, picked my chin up, and started playing this practice game. I did my best, I worked hard, and funnily enough I started playing really well. Because again there

Diary..... of a professional Footballer

was this strange feeling of relief. 'Sod it. I'm out of it.' So I just enjoyed myself for half an hour. And all the time, at the back of my mind, I was wondering 'What am I going to do? How am I going to react? What do I do now?'

Seven games of the season had gone. And after all the struggle, all the worry, all the dreams, you are on the scrapheap. That is what the reserves is, when you are twenty-eight. No one had said a word to me. It was the same as if I had never given a damn. They had treated me as if I had never tried.

And I *had* tried. In the games where Dennis had been out, and there was no one there to take responsibility, I had taken it. I had covered for people, I had worked, I had shouted, I had bawled, I had grafted, I had tackled — which I cannot do very well — I had done all of that. And I was missing Dennis being alongside me doing things, because he takes a lot of that responsibility. I took all that on my own shoulders, tried to do the right thing, tried to do more than my whack, to make up for the fact that he was not there. All the time waiting for him to get back into the side so we could get it organized again. Like we had done in the latter part of last season. It never entered my mind that I might be dropped.

It had, funnily enough, when Franky had been playing so well. I thought 'Well, Dennis is going to come back in, and he just might drop me.' But then I had played well in a couple of games, I had made the goal against Wednesday, and I had pulled well in the first half at Swindon when things were rocky. I had pulled the side together, and I thought I had done very well. So I said to myself 'Now it's OK. You won't be dropped.' I thought he would drop Gordon Hill. I wanted Dennis back in the side.

But he had dropped Gordon Hill and me. And he brought this lad Robin Wainwright in. He has done well in the reserves, and should be given a chance. But he is not a midfield player, he is a winger or a striker.

So I reacted by playing as best I could for the reserves in that practice match. Trying to be manly, trying not to be small-minded. And when we finished I went to see Benny. When I walked through the door he said 'What do you want?'

'You know what I want,' I said. 'I want to leave this place. I want to leave within a week. I'm finished here.'

'Out of the question,' he said. 'You're too good a player.'

So I said 'I don't care why you have dropped me, I don't want to discuss it. Team selection is your business. But I'm finished with it. I have put too much work in, too much commitment, too much caring to be messed around like that. You did not even tell me before that I was dropped. I find out when a guy walks past me with a shirt. That's you, that is this club. No more for me. I'm finished. I want to leave. And if you do not let me leave, I'll leave anyway.'

'Out of the question. Calm yourself down.'

I did not talk about why he had dropped me. I do not believe in discussing team selection with managers. They have got a reason, and whatever the reason is, it is good enough. It is their job. You don't have to take it, if you don't believe it is right.

I was in a terrible temper. My hand was shaking, I could not talk properly. I was hurt more than angry.

So I said 'I'll wait ten days. And if you don't let me go, I'll go anyway. Don't put me on the sheet, don't take me with you.'

'What about the money?'

'You can stuff the money,' I said. 'I don't care about that.'

So I went home. I phoned Sandra first, and told her what had happened. I walked in and just burst out crying. I sat here for quarter of an hour, and I just cried.

I had never cried before about football. Never ever. But this time I did. I don't know why. Maybe it was the hurt, the injustice of it. But that has happened before. Every year, the first sign of the team having problems and it is me he drops. He tells me that he thinks the world of me as a person, but when we lose games the first person he sorts out is me. I do think he likes me. I think the reason he does drop me every time is because of a weakness in him. He is the kind of person who would sooner hurt his friends than his enemies. But I did not think it would happen to me again.

The other lads were surprised. Alan said 'It's scandalous.'

I had not looked for sympathy. When you get dropped, players come up to you and say 'Diabolical.' They always say it whether they mean it or not. But when it happens to me, I try and avoid them. I don't want them to say it, because it does not mean anything. It is not real. What is real is what goes on the teamsheet. The rest is rubbish.

Understanding

1 From the first diary entry of 28 September it is obvious that Dunphy is unhappy with things at his club. Write down what you consider to be his *three* most serious worries.

2 The diary entry for 29 September describes a complete game from one player's point of view. Rewrite the report, but this time as it might appear in the Sunday papers. Invent a suitable headline and try your hand at being an ace sports reporter. For example, your report could begin:

Cheeky Carlisle Mangle Millwall
No one was dancing at the Den this afternoon as Millwall crumbled before a couple of well taken chances from an oh so cheeky Carlisle! A lack lustre first half had seen . . .
Now over to you!

3 When Dunphy learns that he has been dropped from the first team (see the entry for 1 October) his first reaction was 'And I cared! I was part of it.' What do you think he means by this? Explain your answer as fully as you can.

4 Later, at home, he thinks over the reasons why the manager seems to drop him whenever the team is having problems. What conclusion does he come to? How does he attempt to explain the behaviour of the manager and the other players to himself? Write down the conversation he might have with his wife as they discuss these things.

5 Now that you have read these diary entries, what are your feelings towards Eamon Dunphy? What do you make of him as a person and as a professional footballer? Give as many reasons as you can to support your ideas.

Response

1 Write about a time when you have been bitterly disappointed by something. Try to describe how your hopes had been gradually built up, only to be so devastatingly crushed by an unexpected event.

2 Caring about something enough to make a real commitment is very important. Write about a time when you have really cared about something, taken on responsibilities and tried to see it through. What happened?

16

Easy on the Relish

by Andrew Bethell

Binders is an American hamburger chain about to open a new branch in Tooting, London. Claud Tofler, a recent graduate of the 'Hamburger University', is the manager. He employs a mixed bunch of young Londoners, from many different cultural backgrounds. Here he is about to deliver an introductory 'pep' talk to his new recruits:

		(They are interrupted by a blaring sound over the intercom. Tofler has a tannoy system.)
5	**TOFLER**	*(Over the tannoy)* I wanna see all you kids in the preparation area. Now. So move on there.
	RAY	Bloody hell. Worse than a holiday camp.
	BRIAN	He told me room five.
	MILTON	Like school this is.
10	**FRANCIS**	You don't get paid.
	SEBASTIAN	You don't get paid here either. For the first week.
15		*(They begin to move out into the main area. The girls do the same. Leonard sits with his back to the action with his earphones on. Merle hangs back, then stuffs her hat behind a locker.)*
	BARBARA	Hope he's not going to keep us too long. I've got a practice at four.

20	**PHIL**	What star sign are you?
	KIM	Not sure. Taurus, I think.
	PHIL	I could have guessed.

(*Tofler has brought in his own stool. He now stands on it and claps his hands for order.*)

25		
	TOFLER	Hokay there team. Gather round, you hear. Good to see you all in the Binder outfit. Not only is it neat, neat, neat, but you can wear it with pride. That uniform is worn by thousands of youngsters in the U S of A. Like you they're all keen to make their way in the fast food business. Excuse me. Ah. Is it Marlene?
	MERLE	Merle, akshully.
35	**TOFLER**	Well Merle Akshully. Where's your hat, sweetheart? We can't get this game going if you don't have a hat.
	MERLE	I didn't get one.
	TOFLER	Sure you got one Merle. I gave it to you myself.
	MERLE	I didn't get a hat.
	TOFLER	Maybe you lost it. You wanna go look?
	MERLE	You callin' me a liar?
	TOFLER	I just want you to wear the hat, godammit.
45	**MERLE**	I don't have a hat.
	TOFLER	You are foulin' my act here Merle. So we forget the hat. We'll find the hat afterwards. Let's get movin'. Hokay team, who knows what happens Saturday?
50	**COLIN**	Spurs v QPR. Milk Cup, Third Round.
	TOFLER	Nope. More important than that.
	COLIN	Liverpool v Everton . . .
	TOFLER	Hell no. It's the grand opening of the Tooting Binder Bar. And know who's going to be there?
55		
	FRANCIS	JR?
	TOFLER	Nice try, kid.
	FRANCIS	It was a joke.
	TOFLER	No joke. We are privileged to have attendin' our grand openin' ceremonies none other than Mansfield Puckermeyer Junior.
60		

SEBASTIAN	I thought W. C. Fields was dead!
TOFLER	A big man for a big occasion. The grand
65		ceremonial opening of the best Binder Bar
	this side of Tuscaloosa . . .
RAY	Tuscaloosa? Where's that?
TOFLER	Let me finish boy. Tuscaloosa is my home
	town in Alabama. I want this place to be the
70		talk of Tuscaloosa. Lot of people there goin'
	to be rootin' for us. You gonna let em down?

(*Silence*)

	Well are you?
75	**FRANCIS**	Hope not.
TOFLER	'Course you're not. Come Saturday we
	gonna have a team that works so smooth
	it can sell burgers with its eyes shut. So
	po-lite, those customers gonna leave with
80		a smile you could fry eggs on. And so
	damn efficient, we ain't wastin' itty bitty
	nothin'. You hear me? You kids is my
	machine. You with me?
KIM	All the way, sir.
85	**TOFLER**	That's my girl. Now just so's the rest of you
	gonna feel part of the team, I'm gonna
	teach you a cheer. The Binder Cheer. I
	have it printed here on this piece of card.
	I'll read it to you. Give it a try.
90		Goes like this:
	Binder, Binder, we're the best,
	We make burgers, beat the rest.
	We got style,
	We got class,
95		Altogether
	WE KICK ASS.
	And when you get to the last bit you give
	three claps like this. We . . . kick . . . ass.
	Geddit.
100	**LIZA**	Excuse me. I don't understand. What's it
	for? This cheer thing?
TOFLER	Get you psyched up. Now come on team.
	Let's try it.
	Binder, binder . . .

105 | (*A very few feebly try the chant. Leonard,*
| *who finally realised that everyone had left,*
| *walks in at this point. He is baffled.*)

77

Hey, hey, hey, what is this? Give it to me
one time. Let's hear it.
    Binder, Binder, we're the best . . .

110   (*He works hard but the response is even
        feebler than before.*)

Okay so you need a little time to learn it.
So tomorrow it'll be word perfect. I'll put up
these cards in the locker rooms. Give you
115   a chance to familiarise yourselves. Now
before we go onto equipment, I want to
introduce the star system here.

(*He takes out a large name badge.*)

This here is your name badge. You get
120   one of these when you finish your
preliminary training. As you will see it
says: 'Hi, I'm _____' and your name
goes there. Then it says, 'How can I help
you?' And underneath that it says 'My star
125   rating is . . .' Now. Anybody know what
the star rating is?

(*Silence*)

No one got any ideas?
LEONA   At MacDonald's . . .
130 **BARBARA**   You get a star for cheering loud?
TOFLER   Nice try pussycat. You got the idea. You
get stars for makin' an extra special
contribution to the Binder Bar. Cheerin'
good is a start, but you'll need more to
135   earn yourself a star. Exemplary service,
speedy machine operation, high till
turnover. All these will be taken into
consideration. And with a star comes
promotion. If you's on relish, you get to
140   work the frier. If you is on deep freeze, you
get to warm your hands under the infra
red. You catch my meanin'?
LEONA   Incentives, you mean.
TOFLER   You got it Leona, and I wanna tell the rest
145   of you that due to her excellent references
and her previous experience, Leona has
received the first star and thereby
becomes team leader. Let's hear it for
Leona. Hey, hey, hey.

78

150   (*He begins to clap loudly. A few join in.*)

FRANCIS How may stars can you get, Mr Tofler?
TOFLER Well five fit on the badge. Any more than
that boy, an' you'll be runnin' the store.
FRANCIS And how often are they awarded?
155   **TOFLER** End of each month . . . So what you say,
five months?
FRANCIS Could be.
TOFLER Hey, I like it. Ambition. Drive.
Get-up-and-go. I like your style . . .
160   **FRANCIS** Francis, sir.
TOFLER Hokay, so Francis is going for five in five. I
oughta warn you that the Lord giveth, and
the Lord taketh away . . . Any slackness,
like not wearin' a hat, Merle, an' you stand
165   to lose a star.
MERLE I ain't got any stars to lose, 'ave I?
TOFLER No Merle, you have not. From where you
stand there's nowhere to go but out . . .
So we got the star system straight, that's
170   good. Let's get on to this Training
Schedule. You are the A team: Monday
through Wednesday four to eleven,
Thursday through Saturday ten to four.
Hokay, on Fries we have Colin and
175   Philomena.

(*Tofler sounds as if he is introducing a
basketball game. As each pair come
forward they are handed a card of
instructions.*)

180   On Buns we have Sebastian and Kim.
On Grill we have Brian and Barbara and
Ray.
On Preparation we have Francis and Liza
and Milton.
185   On Counter we have Cheryl, Leona,
Majiid and Colin.
On Supplies we have Merle and Leonard.

(*They disperse to the appropriate area
and go to work interpreting the
190   instructions. Tofler circulates. The focus
shifts from group to group.*)

Understanding

1   From the things they say and do, what first impressions do you have of the workforce as they move into the preparation area to hear Tofler speak (the first ten lines of dialogue)? Give reasons for your answer.

2   Once Tofler starts to speak, it becomes clear that he is not totally in tune with the way things usually happen in Britain. List his more important misunderstandings, as you see them (lines 26–67).

3   Lines 68–100 see Tofler placing a great emphasis on 'team' work. In what ways does he do this? Do these methods remind you of anything? Why do you think he places such an emphasis on 'team' work?

4   Tofler's 'star system' is explained on lines 102–166. How does this stress on individual performance fit in with his earlier views on 'team' work? What might Tofler's real motives be with this system?

5   How would you describe the general reaction to Tofler's 'pep' talk? Some seem to react positively. Who are they? In what ways do they show their enthusiasm?

6   Either:
(a) Continue the playscript by following a group or two on 'Fries' 'Buns' or 'Grill', and record their conversations and actions as Tofler circulates amongst them.
Or:
(b) Write Tofler's report after the first full week of operation. He comments on the success or otherwise of the Burger Bar and the suitability of its staff. What might he say to Old Man Binder back in America?

Response

1   Write your own playscript exploring the ways a new style American business approach might change things on, say, Saturday jobs that you are familiar with. Here are some suggested titles: 'Shake Up at the Supermarket'; 'Big Changes at the Chippy'; 'New Approaches to Newspaper Delivery'. What would happen?

17

OveR BReakfast

by Toeckey Jones

Candy took her place at the table and helped herself to toast. She avoided looking at Colin who was sitting directly opposite her.

'Any more tea going?' her father asked after a few moments, reappearing briefly from behind his newspaper.

5 Automatically, Candy picked up his empty cup and passed it across to her mother.

'Pour Dad a cup will you, dear, while I sort through the rest of this mail . . . Why, here's one for you.'

'Me?' Surprised, Candy took the envelope from her mother.
10 Immediately she knew it must be from Becky. Nobody else she knew would have written the address in pencil. Inside was a piece of lined paper which had obviously been torn from an exercise book. She unfolded it on her lap so that Colin, who was watching her curiously, wouldn't be able to read it.

15 'Dear Candy, I hope your ankle is now very well again. Did you take some castor oil? I am writing to you because I have to come to Johannesburg on Saturday to buy more Easter eggs. The other ones got sat on by a fat man in the train going home. It's the truth. He was very cross because the chocolate stuck to his trousers. But it's no
20 matter. He is not a very nice man I think. Some people who know him call him *unwabu* (that means a chameleon) because they say he changes his colour when he talks to the police. They think he is a spy. If you can also come to the city on Saturday, maybe we can meet at the same place in the park. I will look for you there at 11 o'clock (in
25 the morning, hey, not in the evening). *Sala kahle*, Becky Mpala. (*Sala kahle* means *stay well* in Zulu.)'

'Who's your letter from, dear?' Candy's mother asked.

Candy folded the letter and slipped it into its envelope. 'Oh, it's just from the girl I met in town last Saturday,' she said.
30 'Which girl, dear?'

'You know, the one who helped me.'

'You mean the African girl?'

Over Breakfast

'Becky,' Candy said, nodding.

'Oh . . .' Her mother put down her cup. 'Why is she writing to
35   you, dear?'

Candy hesitated. She hadn't yet spoken to her mother about the Zulu lessons and about Becky visiting their house. She had been waiting to catch her in the right mood, and breakfast was not a good time, especially with Colin there. She knew how he would react to the
40   idea.

But her mother was looking at her expectantly, so Candy said, 'She's written to find out how my ankle is.'

'Really? How very thoughtful of her.'

Candy shrugged. 'She seems a very nice girl.'
45   'What did you say her name was again?'

'Becky. It's short for Rebecca.'

'And she's the one who helped you when you fell?'

'If it wasn't for her, I'd probably have been trampled to death,' Candy exaggerated.
50   Her mother shook her head sadly. 'People just don't care any more, do they?'

'Becky did,' Candy was quick to point out.

'Yes, well . . .' Her mother brightened. 'One can draw heart from that, at least. It does seem to show that this dratted government
55   of ours hasn't totally succeeded in destroying all signs of goodwill between the races.'

Candy saw her chance. But still she hesitated, glancing uncertainly at Colin. He was leaning forward on the table, his head down, apparently absorbed in the latest issue of a sports magazine he
60   subscribed to. Her father seemed to be similarly engrossed in his newspaper. Suddenly, Candy thought how ridiculous it was to be nervous of saying that she was going to see Becky again; as if she was admitting to something slightly shameful. Apart from anything else, it was an insult to Becky's trust in impulsively declaring the two of them
65   to be friends. That decided Candy.

In a firm voice, she said, 'Actually, Becky also wrote to suggest meeting me again in town on Saturday.'

'Oh.' Her mother looked surprised. 'Why does she want to do that?'
70   'It was my idea in the first place. *I* wanted to see her again. I asked her to write to me so we could fix up a time.' Candy raised her chin defiantly and stared straight into her mother's eyes. 'I've also asked her to teach me Zulu.'

Her mother lowered her gaze and began flicking through the
75   small pile of opened mail lying next to her plate. 'That's very nice, dear,' she said distantly.

Candy watched her, waiting. Finally, her mother looked up frowning, and took off her reading glasses.

'You've asked this girl to teach you Zulu?'

80 'That's right. She's an ideal person, being a Zulu herself. It's tremendous luck to have found someone suitable at last. She offered to teach me for nothing, but obviously I must pay her. I've been wanting to talk to you about that.' Candy paused hopefully. As her mother remained silent, she went on, 'I could pay for the lessons out

85 of my pocket money, if you like.'

She saw her mother glance towards her father, but he remained hidden behind his newspaper. 'Perhaps Becky could teach you Zulu as well, Mum,' she suggested cunningly. Her mother was always saying how much she wished she could speak an African language.

90 Her mother laughed. 'I'm much too old now to start learning a new language. My brains have become far too addled after all these years.'

'Nonsense!' Candy grinned. 'You should think about it serious-ly. But anyway, you can always see how I get on first. I want to start as

95 soon as possible.' She pushed her plate away and leaned back in her chair, trying to project a cheerful confidence she was far from feeling.

It was obvious that her mother was being evasive. Candy had a nasty feeling that the next few minutes were going to be even more difficult than she had suspected. However, now she had got this far,

100 she knew she had to go on. It was better to get the whole thing over and done with as soon as possible.

Her mother, meanwhile, had started fiddling with the pile of mail again. Extracting a bill, she pretended to study it in great detail, her brow furrowed in exaggerated concentration. Candy stared at her

105 until she had to look up.

'Well . . . ?' Candy asked.

'Well what, dear?'

'Don't you think it's a good idea, my having Zulu lessons?'

'Of course I do, dear. I think it's an excellent idea, if you're really

110 serious about it. Only . . .' Her mother smiled a little anxiously.

'Only?' Candy prompted.

'Well, how can you be sure this girl would be able to teach you properly? I mean it's not as if you know her at all, do you?'

'I've told you she's a Zulu, which is the important thing. I also

115 know she's intelligent, that she's interesting to talk to and that I like her and want to get to know her better. Isn't that enough?'

Her mother nodded doubtfully. 'And where would she teach you?'

Candy swallowed. 'That's one of the things I wanted to talk to

120 you about. Obviously she would have to come here. There's really

Over Breakfast

no other place where we could meet in privacy. I was thinking we
could have the lessons in my bedroom — we wouldn't disturb
anybody there. But I'd really need to have a lesson every week,
otherwise I wouldn't make much progress.'

125   A sudden silence fell over the table. Candy was aware that her
father had stopped reading, although his newspaper remained
raised, shielding his face from her view. Nobody moved. Then Colin
turned over a page of his magazine and casually went on reading, and
Candy breathed out in relief to know that he, at least, seemed
130 unaware of what she had said.

    Her mother began picking crumbs off the cloth in quick, nervous
movements. 'I don't know, dear,' she said. 'I really don't know. I
mean I'm not even sure the law allows it.' She glanced desperately at
her husband, but the newspaper blocked her appeal for help. Raising
135 her voice, she asked, 'Is it legal, Ron, do you know?'

    There was a pause, and then Candy's father laid the paper aside
irritably.

    'Don't ask me,' he said. 'As far as I know, you can have Africans
visit you so long as you don't offer them liquor.'

140   'There's no problem then.' Candy gave a feeble grin. 'I
shouldn't think Becky would expect anything stronger than tea.'

    'It's not all that simple and straightforward, dear.' Her mother
shifted uncomfortably in her chair. 'There are the neighbours to
consider. I mean, what are they going to say when they find out you
145 have a black friend visiting you regularly on a . . .'

    'Bugger the neighbours.'

    '*What* did you say?'

    Candy turned and looked at her father in nervous, silent
defiance.

150   'I won't have you talking that way to your mother,' he warned.
Angrily, he picked up his newspaper and hid behind it once more.

Understanding

1   **What was it about the letter which made Candy
immediately think it was from Becky? Is there anything else
about the way the letter is described (lines 10–26) which
might suggest something about its sender?**

2   Read again the letter from Becky. In it she refers to a fat man as '*unwabu* (that means chameleon)' because 'he changes his colour when he talks to the police'. What do you think Becky means by this remark?

3   Pay particular attention to the times when Colin is mentioned in this extract. How is he described on these occasions? Make a list of some of the words used. What do these words tell you about Candy's feelings towards Colin?

4   Between lines 97 and 110 the mother behaves in a rather peculiar way. Make a list of the things she does. What do these actions tell you about her real thoughts and feelings at this time?

5   The father continues with his newspaper right to the end of the extract. Why do you think he hides in this way? And why was he so irritated by the conversation between his wife and daughter?

6   Either:
(a) Candy decides to go to her room, leaving her father, mother and Colin still at the table. The three of them start to discuss what has just taken place with Candy. Write down the conversation you think they would have.
Or:
(b) Candy replies to Becky's letter and attempts to describe the breakfast time discussion. Write out the letter you think Candy would send.

Response

1   Write about a time when a friend of yours was 'strongly disapproved of' by your parents. What happened?

2   Disagreements within families can take many forms. Sometimes small acts or gestures and very few words can conceal raging torrents of feeling, just below the surface. Describe a family event, perhaps similar to the breakfast scene in the extract, where major differences exist but where those involved struggle to retain some self-control and try to resist, not always successfully, the slide into an all out shouting match!

18

A Polished Performance

by D J Enright

Citizens of the polished capital
    Sigh for the towns up country,
And their innocent simplicity.

People in the towns up country
    Applaud the unpolished innocence
Of the distant villages.

Dwellers in the distant villages
    Speak of a simple unspoilt girl,
Living alone, deep in the bush.

Deep in the bush we found her,
    Large and innocent of eye,
Among gentle gibbons and mountain ferns.

Perfect for the part, perfect,
    Except for the dropsy
Which comes from polished rice.

In the capital our film is much admired,
    Its gentle gibbons and mountain ferns,
Unspoilt, unpolished, large and innocent of eye.

Understanding

1   First copy out the poem on a separate piece of paper. Read it through carefully, several times, looking for words, phrases or ideas that *connect* with one another. Underline these connecting words or link them with pencil in some way.

2   Where is this poem set? Give reasons for your answer.

3   Describe, as best you can, what you feel to be happening as the poem moves through verses one and two to three. What do these three verses have to do with making a film?

4   Using your own words, what sense do you make of the unexpected twist in verse five?

5   Why might the film be especially admired 'in the capital' (verse six)? What do you make of the repetition of certain words already used in verse four?

6   Now that you have read and considered the poem in full, what do you think the writer was suggesting by his choice of title: 'A Polished Performance'?

7   The finished film is about to open in 'the capital'.
    Either:
    (a) Write a favourable press review from a person sympathetic to the aims of the film crew.
    Or:
    (b) Write a critical review by someone angered by the film crew's selectivity and false sentiment.

Response

1   Try reversing the whole sequence of events suggested by this poem and see what happens. Something, an idea, an incident or a person, moves from the distant villages through the up country towns and, only finally, reaches the capital. On arrival it turns out to be quite different from what was originally expected and, as a consequence, many people are shocked and disturbed. Write about what might happen, either as a poem or as a short story.

19

The Distant One

by Michael Anthony

It didn't seem such a long time that Albert was away. At least not a year. How the months had flown! A year since Albert was packing, since . . .

5 The boy sat up on the bed with the scene vivid in his mind. He relived all the excitement, and pain, and the emptiness of the days that followed: they all came back to his mind this morning. Really, they had never left him. But this morning the pain cut deeper, and the emptiness was more complete.

The other members of the household, though, were up and 10 stirring. The other children had already changed from their night clothes, and were getting busy as usual. The mother hurried about the house, sweeping, dusting, and dashing into and out of the kitchen. Once or twice she glanced from the corner of her eyes at the little boy sitting there on the bed. Now she glanced again and he was 15 still there. 'I wonder what's Leroy's intention this morning!' she said aloud, half of herself, and half sharply; but she went about her chores.

Leroy had indeed been day-dreaming. If any sound came to him it must have come from far away. For his own spinning top was in his mind's eye.

20 He was recalling the very morning that top was made. He could see Albert now, bending over the lagnette wood, chopping, chopping, until gradually — almost magically — a brand new top was born. Then Albert had taken a nail from his pocket, moved over the fireplace to heat it, and as easily as ever he had made the hot nail go 25 into the wood. He had got the exact depth, then he put the top in water to cool the nail off. Then he had said, 'Here, Lee, try it out!' And Albert had watched Lee put on the marling twine, and when he had released the top from the twine with a zing, they were both amazed to see how perfectly it spun, and for him it was the best top in the world.

30 'It's yours, Lee!' Albert had said then. Leroy had been so surprised and glad that words failed to come. From that moment it had come home to him that he and Albert were real, real pals, closer than anything.

All these thoughts were flooding back to him now and he was 35 completely carried away.

'Leroy!'

The mother's voice was sharp, almost thunderous, so that the boy, completely startled, felt his heart jump. But the next moment he had regained his senses and was now hustling out of his pyjamas and
40   hurrying into some clothes.

The mother did not have to say any more because Leroy's task was clear cut.

He was out into the yard now. He hurried to the goats — for he should have already been on his way to the tethering place — and
45   though the top was in his pocket, this morning there would be no time for a *one-line* game.

The morning sun had already struck the pitch road. He felt the surface warm and pleasant to his feet. The goats must have felt the same, for instead of walking on the roadside grass, they walked in the
50   centre of the road. Albert had never pulled them away when they walked in the centre of the road. Only when a car came hurtling up. And in the evening when he went for them again he did not have to lead them for they knew the house and were anxious. And they trusted Albert. When he stood up they stood up, too, and when he
55   started again they started. And now the goats were here and Albert was not here, and the sun made it warm underfoot. That was funny. The boy smiled wistfully to himself, and he could not help wondering whether the sun made it warm under Albert's feet, too, this morning, wherever he was in that England place.

60   It was different when the last letter had come. Albert had said it was not too bad but it was cold. He had mentioned that there was so much to see and so many places to go to, and it would have been very nice had it not been cold. And then he wrote to ask about Leroy. With this thought the boy felt a sharp pain, which, though he was not tired,
65   made his breath come in gasps. He remembered the letter vividly for he had taken it to school with him and must have read it a hundred times. He and his friends. He had been so proud, but now it was already a long time.

He must write to Albert. He had tried several times but whenever
70   he took up the pen he could not find words to say. But he must write. For Meggy had kids again, and one had died. And the mango trees in Spring Flat were yellow with fruit. And the top — he hung his head, for he would not tell about the nail-hole — the top was still good and he wouldn't play *one-line* with it!

75   Were it not for the goats he might have walked on past the savannah. But the goats turned off the road, almost dragging him with them. 'Scamps!' he said, as if he realised they had a point on him. And he looked for where the grass was greenest and began driving in his stakes.

The Distant One

80   The mother tried to be her usual self in spite of everything. She was always up and doing, busy as ever about the house. She made it a point of duty to be so. For she realised that not only did she have to take Albert off the children's mind but off her own mind as well. She could not have carried on if she had allowed the terrible longing to

85   take possession of her. The boy had gone away for a few years only. He had been determined to go and he had worked and had saved his own money. She hoped he made good there because she had counted on his coming back and helping her with the smaller ones. And naturally she was longing to see him again. In the first place, it

90   was not easy letting him go.

    She always thought of him but she had fought hard to suppress her feelings. Especially in the light of the children, and particularly so in the light of Leroy, who, if given a moment to himself, would fall into brooding and dream.

95   She roused herself from her thoughts. Was she not dreaming, too? She busied herself sweeping out the house and then she went outside to wash some clothes. Then she went in and took up the shopbag as she heard the drone of the mail-bus. She would go to the shop first, then in coming back she would look in at the Post Office.

100   She would not have to go in for she was sure the lady in the Post Office would look out and signal 'No'. Or maybe . . . who knows?

    As it turned out the lady in the Post Office looked out and signalled 'No'. The mother turned back with pain and took the road up the hill. Seeing that she was broken-spirited the lady in the Post Office called

105   out, 'Perhaps tomorrow, Mrs Austin'.

    Mrs Austin turned back and forced a smile. 'Perhaps. I'll send the little boy.'

    There were no letters that week. Nor the next week, nor the next. But some time in the following week the postmistress looked out for when

110   the boy was passing and hailed to him and signalled to him to come.

    The boy ran up the road gingerly, and received the letter, and both he and the postmistress laughed. Then he sped up the hill to his home.

    The family huddled together to read the letter. The children,

115   including Leroy, read with difficulty, because the words were long and they had not learnt them yet. But it was not long before the mother finished and she went back to the kitchen. Then she went back out to the children and she said, 'I don't think he said exactly when he'll come but it won't be long now. Let me see . . .' She took

120   the letter away and went into the kitchen. And she said to herself: 'Oh, is so? England nice. Trinidad too backward. He playing man already. Okay, let him stay there. We'll live without him.' And she called out, 'Leroy, go and give the goats water!'

Understanding

1   The first 35 lines of this story provide a reader with a lot of information about Leroy as a character. Read through the list of words which follow and select three which best describe Leroy as you see him: fun-loving, lazy, sad, hard-working, thoughtful, friendly, intelligent, lonely, jealous.

      Then, referring back to the story, give as many reasons as you can to support your three choices.

2   Stories always carry information, but sometimes it is more enjoyable to a reader if facts are gently suggested rather than boldly stated. Carefully re-read lines 43–59, then make a list of all the facts you have discovered about Leroy's way of life.

3   What evidence is there in the story that Albert's letters meant a lot to Leroy?

4   Lines 80–105 describe the mother in some detail. But how would you describe her as a woman? Try to support your points with evidence from the story.

5   The story is titled 'The Distant One'. Invent an alternative title which still seems to fit the mood and atmosphere of the piece. What would it be? Give reasons for your final choice.

6   Either:
(a) As readers, we are never told the exact content of that last letter from Albert. Write out what you think that letter might have contained.
Or:
(b) Leroy goes out to give 'the goats water', leaving his mother with her older children. Write down their conversation as they talk about Albert and his letter.

Response

1   On several occasions in the story, Leroy was 'completely carried away' by the thoughts and memories that were 'flooding back to him'. Describe a time when thoughts or day-dreams have carried you away to a place where no one else can reach you.

2   Time spent away from home can be a difficult time for all concerned. Write about just such a family separation, for whatever reason, in the way you think best.

by POSY SIMMONDS

ALWAYS IN THE NEWS....

Understanding

1 What is the common thread linking all seven news reports featured in this cartoon strip? In what way is this link reflected in the title of the strip?

2 As the news reports are read out, one after the other, the reactions of the women present seem to change. How would you describe this gradual change across the eight frames of the cartoon?

3 Similarly, changes are clearly affecting the single male present! Taking the cartoon frame by frame, describe in your own words the series of physical reactions he has to the evening's news stories. What do you feel the cartoonist is suggesting through these changes? What point is she trying to make?

4 How successful do you feel the cartoon is in getting across its message? Did it make you think again? What effect would it have on other people of your age? What sort of people would like it, dislike or misunderstand it? Give as many reasons for your answer as you can.

Response

1 Your family is together, watching the news on television when, suddenly, something comes on which either infuriates or seriously embarrasses you. What do you do? What do the others do? Write out what might happen as a short playscript or perhaps as a 'seriously comic' cartoon strip in the style of Posy Simmonds.

2 Are cartoons or comic strips suitable for exploring serious issues? Collect a few examples, and, by examining them closely, try to decide just how successful they are as vehicles for comment, criticism or debate.

21

GUTTER
by Paul Dehn

NEWS EDITOR   Peer Confesses,
Bishop Undresses,
Torso Wrapped In Rug,
Girl Guide Throttled
5   Baronet Bottled,
J.P. Goes To Jug.

But yesterday's story's
Old and hoary.
Never mind who got hurt.
10   No use grieving,
Let's get weaving.
What's the latest dirt?

Diplomat Spotted,
Scout Garrotted,
15   Thigh Discovered In Bog,
Wrecks Off Barmouth,
Sex In Yarmouth,
Women In Love With Dog,
Eminent Hostess Shoots Her Guests,
20   Harrogate Lovebird Builds Two Nests.

CAMERAMAN   Builds two nests?
Shall I get a picture of the lovebird singing?
Shall I get a picture of her pretty little eggs?
Shall I get a picture of her babies?

PRESS

25	**NEWS EDITOR**	No! Go and get a picture of her legs.
		Beast Slays Beauty,
		Priest Flays Cutie,
		Cupboard Shows Tell-Tale Stain,
		Mate Drugs Purser,
30		Dean Hugs Bursar,
		Mayor Binds Wife With Chain,
		Elderly Actress Marries For Money,
		Jilted Crooner Says 'I Want Ma Honey'.
	CAMERAMAN	'Want ma honey?'
35		Shall I get a picture of the pollen flying?
		Shall I get a picture of the golden dust?
		Shall I get a picture of a queen bee?
	NEWS EDITOR	No! Go and get a picture of her bust.
		Judge Gets Frisky,
40		Nun Drinks Whisky,
		Baby Found Burnt In Cot,
		Show Girl Beaten,
		Duke Leaves Eton —
	CAMERAMAN	Newspaper Man Gets Shot!
45		May all things clean
		And fresh and green
		Have mercy upon your soul,
		Consider yourself paid
		By the hole my bullet made —
50	**NEWS EDITOR**	Come and get a picture of the hole.
	[*dying*]	

95

GUTTER PRESS

Understanding

1   Look again at the lines spoken by the News Editor. Where have you seen lines like these before? Why is it so easy to identify their source?

2   In what ways do lines 7–12 help you to make sense of the six lines immediately above and the eight immediately below?

3   The language used by the News Editor is very different from that used by the Cameraman. How many differences can you find? Why might these differences be important?

4   The Cameraman's first two reactions to his editor (lines 21–24 and 34–38) are similar in many respects. How would you describe these reactions and their similarities?

5   The News Editor's replies (lines 25–33 and 38–43) also suggest a certain approach to people and events. How would you describe this approach?

6   The Cameraman's third reaction however (lines 44–49) is very different. How do you account for this sudden change? What in particular do you think he means by lines 45 and 46?

Response

1   Try out some Editor/Cameraman conversations of your own. You may need to read a selection of newspapers first to gain inspiration. Then follow the pattern suggested by the poem above but with your own variations and additions.

22

SAMUEL

by Grace Paley

Some boys are very tough. They're afraid of nothing. They are the ones who climb a wall and take a bow at the top. Not only are they brave on the roof, but they make a lot of noise in the darkest part of the cellar where even the super hates to go. They also jiggle and hop
5   on the platform between the locked doors of the subway cars.

Four boys are jiggling on the swaying platform. Their names are Alfred, Calvin, Samuel, and Tom. The men and the women in the cars on either side watch them. They don't like them to jiggle or jump but don't want to interfere. Of course some of the men in the cars
10   were once brave boys like these. One of them had ridden the tail of a speeding truck from New York to Rockaway Beach without getting off, without his sore fingers losing hold. Nothing happened to him then or later. He had made a compact with other boys who preferred to watch; starting at Eighth Avenue and Fifteenth Street, he would get
15   to some specified place, maybe Twenty-third and the river, by hopping the tops of the moving trucks. This was hard to do when one truck turned a corner in the wrong direction and the nearest truck was a couple of feet too high. He made three or four starts before succeeding. He had gotten this idea from a film at school called *The*
20   *Romance of Logging.* He had finished high school, married a good friend, was in a responsible job and going to night school.

These two men and others looked at the four boys jumping and jiggling on the platform and thought, It must be fun to ride that way, especially now the weather is nice and we're out of the tunnel and
25   way high over the Bronx. Then they thought, These kids do seem to be acting sort of stupid. They *are* little. Then they thought of some of the brave things they had done when they were boys and jiggling didn't seem so risky.

The ladies in the car became very angry when they looked at the
30   four boys. Most of them brought their brows together and hoped the boys could see their extreme disapproval. One of the ladies wanted to get up and say, Be careful you dumb kids, get off that platform or I'll call a cop. But three of the boys were Negroes and the fourth was something else she couldn't tell for sure. She was afraid they'd be
35   fresh and laugh at her and embarrass her. She wasn't afraid they'd hit

SAMUEL

her, but she was afraid of embarrassment. Another lady thought, Their mothers never know where they are. It wasn't true in this particular case. Their mothers all knew that they had gone to see the missile exhibit on Fourteenth Street.

40   Out on the platform, whenever the train accelerated, the boys would raise their hands and point them up to the sky to act like rockets going off, then they rat-tat-tatted the shatterproof glass pane like machine guns, although no machine guns had been exhibited.

For some reason known only to the motorman, the train began a
45   sudden slowdown. The lady who was afraid of embarrassment saw the boys jerk forward and backward and grab the swinging guard chains. She had her own boy at home. She stood up with determination and went to the door. She slid it open and said, 'You boys will be hurt. You'll be killed. I'm going to call the conductor if
50   you don't just go into the next car and sit down and be quiet.'

Two of the boys said, 'Yes'm,' and acted as though they were about to go. Two of them blinked their eyes a couple of times and pressed their lips together. The train resumed its speed. The door slid shut, parting the lady and the boys. She leaned against the side door
55   because she had to get off at the next stop.

The boys opened their eyes wide at each other and laughed. The lady blushed. The boys looked at her and laughed harder. They began to pound each other's back. Samuel laughed the hardest and pounded Alfred's back until Alfred coughed and the tears came.
60   Alfred held tight to the chain hook. Samuel pounded him even harder when he saw the tears. He said, 'Why you bawling? You a baby, huh?' and laughed. One of the men whose boyhood had been more watchful than brave became angry. He stood up straight and looked at the boys for a couple of seconds. Then he walked in a
65   citizenly way to the end of the car, where he pulled the emergency cord. Almost at once, with a terrible hiss, the pressure of air abandoned the brakes and the wheels were caught and held.

People standing in the most secure places fell forward, then backward. Samuel had let go of his hold on the chain so he could
70   pound Tom as well as Alfred. All the passengers in the cars whipped back and forth, but he pitched only forward and fell head first to be crushed and killed between the cars.

98

The train had stopped hard, halfway into the station, and the conductor called at once for the trainmen who knew about this kind
75 of death and how to take the body from the wheels and brakes. There was silence except for passengers from other cars who asked, What happened! What happened! The ladies waited around wondering if he might be an only child. The men recalled other afternoons with very bad endings. The little boys stayed close to each other, leaning
80 and touching shoulders and arms and legs.

When the policeman knocked at the door and told her about it, Samuel's mother began to scream. She screamed all day and moaned all night, though the doctors tried to quiet her with pills.

Oh, oh, she hopelessly cried. She did not know how she could
85 ever find another boy like that one. However, she was a young woman and she became pregnant. Then for a few months she was hopeful. The child born to her was a boy. They brought him to be seen and nursed. She smiled. But immediately she saw that this baby wasn't Samuel. She and her husband together have had other
90 children, but never again will a boy exactly like Samuel be known.

Understanding

1   'Four boys are jiggling on the swaying platform . . . The men
    and the women in the cars on either side watch them.' Lines
    8–28 describe some of the thoughts going through the
    men's minds as they watch. Lines 29–55 describe some of
    the reactions of the women.

    Divide your page into two and using your own words, list
    all the male responses on one side, and all the female on the
    other. How many differences can you find?

2   The man who eventually pulls the emergency cord is described as 'one of the men whose boyhood had been more watchful than brave' who 'stood up straight' and walked 'in a citizenly way' towards the emergency cord. From these brief descriptions, what sort of a man do you consider him to be? Give reasons for your answer.

3   Samuel's mother was young and went on to have other children but 'never again will a boy exactly like Samuel be known'. What do you understand by this statement?

4   Which of the following statements gets closest to what you consider the story to be mainly about? Read them through carefully and then place them in your order of preference, giving as many reasons as you can for your selection.
    (a) This is a story which is mainly interested in the way youngsters are prepared to risk their lives just for fun and excitement.
    (b) This is a story which is mainly concerned with the different ways boys and girls are brought up in American society.
    (c) This is a story about an interfering busy-body who is really responsible for causing Samuel's death.
    (d) This is a story which brings home the difference between romantic, 'story-book' notions of danger and excitement and their often grim and tragic realities.

Response

1   'Tales Of Excitement And Adventure For Boys'
    Vs
    'Stories Of Love And Romance For Girls'
    Attempt to break through these false alternatives with a story of your own which either: shows girls involved in exciting and daring tasks, or demonstrates that boys can show affection and care for others.

2   Write about a time when you have observed somebody doing something they should not be doing. Describe your thoughts and feelings as you decided whether or not to interfere.

23

Understanding

1   After studying both Judge Dredd cartoons, consider these
    five statements:

    (a) Judge Dredd is an effective law enforcer, whose ends
         justify his means.
    (b) Judge Dredd is an authoritarian with no respect for a
         citizen's rights or democratic procedures.
    (c) Judge Dredd puts across simple moral truths in a
         powerful way which anyone can understand.
    (d) Judge Dredd dangerously over-simplifies social
         problems and is likely to do more harm than good.
    (e) Judge Dredd is just a comic book character and should
         not be taken too seriously.

    Take each statement in turn and, in as much detail as you
    can, write down your reactions and thoughts to the points
    being made. Support your ideas by referring, whenever
    possible, to examples from the cartoon strips.

2   Finally, select the statement you agree with most strongly as
    well as the statement you disagree with the most. Give
    reasons for your selection.

3   How would you answer the charge that the 'Judge Dredd
    comics represent all the worst aspects of American society
    and therefore should not be allowed in British schools'. On
    the evidence of these two strips, where do you stand?

Response

1   Invent your own Judge Dredd episode on a suitable theme
    such as cruelty to animals, environmental pollution, drug
    abuse. You could illustrate your ideas in cartoon form or
    describe what you would like to see in words, taking each
    frame at a time. (See 'Robot on the Rampage' page 21 if you
    wish to try a more ambitious 'shooting script' approach.)

Judgement on Judge Dredd

by John Wagner and Ron Smith

24

Next Term We'll Mash You

by Penelope Lively

Inside the car it was quiet, the noise of the engine even and subdued, the air just the right temperature, the windows tight-fitting. The boy sat on the back seat, a box of chocolates, unopened, beside him, and a comic, folded. The trim Sussex landscape flowed past the windows:
5   cows, white-fenced fields, highly-priced period houses. The sunlight was glassy, remote as a coloured photograph. The backs of the two heads in front of him swayed with the motion of the car.

His mother half-turned to speak to him. 'Nearly there now, darling.'
10   The father glanced downwards at his wife's wrist. 'Are we all right for time?'

'Just right. Nearly twelve.'

'I could do with a drink. Hope they lay something on.'

'I'm sure they will. The Wilcoxes say they're awfully nice people.
15 Not really the schoolmaster-type at all, Sally says.'

The man said, 'He's an Oxford chap.'

'Is he? You didn't say.'

'Mmn.'

'Of course, the fees are that much higher than the Seaford
20 place.'

'Fifty quid or so. We'll have to see.'

The car turned right, between white gates and high, dark, tight-clipped hedges. The whisper of the road under the tyres changed to the crunch of gravel. The child, staring sideways, read
25 black lettering on a white board: 'St Edward's Preparatory School. Please Drive Slowly'. He shifted on the seat, and the leather sucked at the bare skin under his knees, stinging.

The mother said, 'It's a lovely place. Those must be the playing-fields. Look, darling, there are some of the boys.' She clicked
30 open her handbag, and the sun caught her mirror and flashed in the child's eyes; the comb went through her hair and he saw the grooves it left, neat as distant ploughing.

'Come on, then, Charles, out you get.'

The building was red brick, early nineteenth century, spreading out long arms in which windows glittered blackly. Flowers, trapped in neat beds, were alternate red and white. They went up the steps, the man, the woman, and the child two paces behind.

The woman, the mother, smoothing down a skirt that would be ridged from sitting, thought: I like the way they've got the maid all done up properly. The little white apron and all that. She's foreign, I suppose. Au pair. Very nice. If he comes here there'll be Speech Days and that kind of thing. Sally Wilcox says it's quite dressy — she got that cream linen coat for coming down here. You can see why it costs a bomb. Great big grounds and only an hour and a half from London.

They went into a room looking out into a terrace. Beyond, dappled lawns, gently shifting trees, black and white cows grazing behind iron railings. Books, leather chairs, a table with magazines — *Country Life, The Field, The Economist.* 'Please, if you would wait here. The Headmaster won't be long.'

Alone, they sat, inspected. 'I like the atmosphere, don't you, John?'

'Very pleasant, yes.' Four hundred a term, near enough. You can tell it's a cut above the Seaford place, though, or the one at St Albans. Bob Wilcox says quite a few City people send their boys here. One or two of the merchant bankers, those kind of people. It's the sort of contact that would do no harm at all. You meet someone, get talking at a cricket match or what have you . . . Not at all a bad thing.

'All right, Charles? You didn't get sick in the car, did you?'

The child had black hair, slicked down smooth to his head. His ears, too large, jutted out, transparent in the light from the window, laced with tiny, delicate veins. His clothes had the shine and crease of newness. He looked at the books, the dark brown pictures, his parents, said nothing.

'Come here, let me tidy your hair.'

The door opened. The child hesitated, stood up, sat, then rose again with his father.

'Mr and Mrs Manders? How very nice to meet you — I'm Margaret Spokes, and will you please forgive my husband who is tied up with some wretch who broke the cricket pavilion window and will be just a few more minutes. We try to be organised but a schoolmaster's day is always just that bit unpredictable. Do please sit down and what will you have to revive you after that beastly drive? You live in Finchley, is that right?'

'Hampstead, really,' said the mother. 'Sherry would be lovely.'

She worked over the headmaster's wife from shoes to hairstyle, pricing and assessing. Shoes old but expensive — Russell and

NEXT TERM WE'LL MASH YOU

Bromley. Good skirt. Blouse could be Marks and Sparks — not sure. Real pearls. Super Victorian ring. She's not gone to any particular trouble — that's just what she'd wear anyway. You can be confident, with a voice like that, of course. Sally Wilcox says she knows all sorts of people.

The headmaster's wife said, 'I don't know how much you know about us. Prospectuses don't tell you a thing, do they? We'll look round everything in a minute, when you've had a chat with my husband. I gather you're friends of the Wilcoxes, by the way. I'm awfully fond of Simon — he's down for Winchester, of course, but I expect you know that.'

The mother smiled over her sherry. Oh, I know that all right. Sally Wilcox doesn't let you forget that.

'And this is Charles? My dear, we've been forgetting all about you! In a minute I'm going to borrow Charles and take him off to meet some of the boys because after all you're choosing a school for him, aren't you, and not for you, so he ought to know what he might be letting himself in for and it shows we've got nothing to hide.'

The parents laughed. The father, sherry warming his guts, thought that this was an amusing woman. Not attractive, of course, a bit homespun, but impressive all the same. Partly the voice, of course; it takes a bloody expensive education to produce a voice like that. And other things, of course. Background and all that stuff.

'I think I can hear the thud of the Fourth Form coming in from games, which means my husband is on the way, and then I shall leave you with him while I take Charles off to the common-room.'

For a moment the three adults centred on the child, looking, judging. The mother said, 'He looks so hideously pale, compared to those boys we saw outside.'

'My dear, that's London, isn't it? You just have to get them out, to get some colour into them. Ah, here's James. James — Mr and Mrs Manders. You remember, Bob Wilcox was mentioning at Sports Day . . .'

The headmaster reflected his wife's style, like paired cards in Happy Families. His clothes were mature rather than old, his skin well-scrubbed, his shoes clean, his geniality untainted by the least condescension. He was genuinely sorry to have kept them waiting, but in this business one lurches from one minor crisis to the next . . . And this is Charles? Hello, there, Charles. His large hand rested for a moment on the child's head, quite extinguishing the thin, dark hair. It was as though he had but to clench his fingers to crush the skull. But he took his hand away and moved the parents to the window, to observe the mutilated cricket pavilion, with indulgent laughter.

120 And the child is borne away by the headmaster's wife. She never touches him or tells him to come, but simply bears him away like some relentless tide, down corridors and through swinging glass doors, towing him like a frail craft, not bothering to look back to see if he is following, confident in the strength of magnetism, or obedience.

125 And delivers him to a room where boys are scattered among inky tables and rungless chairs and sprawled on a mangy carpet. There is a scampering, and a rising, and a silence falling, as she opens the door.

'Now this is the Lower Third, Charles, who you'd be with if you

130 come to us in September. Boys, this is Charles Manders, and I want you to tell him all about things and answer any questions he wants to ask. You can believe about half of what they say, Charles, and they will tell you the most fearful lies about the food, which is excellent.'

The boys laugh and groan; amiable, exaggerated groans. They

135 must like the headmaster's wife: there is licensed repartee. They look at her with bright eyes in open, eager faces. Someone leaps to hold the door for her, and close it behind her. She is gone.

The child stands in the centre of the room, and it draws in around him. The circle of children contracts, faces are only a yard or so from

140 him; strange faces, looking, assessing.

Asking questions. They help themselves to his name, his age, his school. Over their heads he sees beyond the window an inaccessible world of shivering trees and high racing clouds and his voice which has floated like a feather in the dusty schoolroom air dies altogether

145 and he becomes mute, and he stands in the middle of them with shoulders humped, staring down at feet: grubby plimsolls and kicked brown sandals. There is a noise in his ears like rushing water, a torrential din out of which voices boom, blotting each other out so that he cannot always hear the words. Do you? they say, and Have

150 you? and What's your? and the faces, if he looks up, swing into one another in kaleidoscopic patterns and the floor under his feet is unsteady, lifting and falling.

And out of the noises comes one voice that is complete, that he can hear. 'Next term, we'll mash you,' it says. 'We always mash new

155 boys.'

And a bell goes, somewhere beyond doors and down corridors, and suddenly the children are all gone, clattering away and leaving him there with the heaving floor and the walls that shift and swing, and the headmaster's wife comes back and tows him away, and he is

160 with his parents again, and they are getting into the car, and the high

NEXT TERM WE'LL MASH YOU

hedges skim past the car windows once more, in the other direction, and the gravel under the tyres changes to black tarmac.

'Well?'

'I liked it, didn't you?' The mother adjusted the car around her,
165 closing windows, shrugging into her seat.

'Very pleasant, really. Nice chap.'

'I liked him. Not quite so sure about her.'

'It's pricey, of course.'

'All the same . . .'
170 'Money well spent, though. One way and another.'

'Shall we settle it, then?'

'I think so. I'll drop him a line.'

The mother pitched her voice a notch higher to speak to the child in the back of the car. 'Would you like to go there, Charles? Like
175 Simon Wilcox. Did you see that lovely gym, and the swimming-pool? And did the other boys tell you all about it?'

The child does not anwer. He looks straight ahead of him, at the road coiling beneath the bonnet of the car. His face is haggard with anticipation.

Understanding

1   Read the first seven lines again closely. List as much evidence as you can find within these lines which suggest the kind of social and financial background the boy in the car might have.

2   Lines 38–51 describe the thoughts and feelings of the mother as she enters the school. From all that you read here, what do you consider to be the real reasons for her wanting to send her son to this particular school?

3   The headmaster's wife delivers Charles to the lower third (line 129). What differences do you immediately notice between the world of the lower third and that of the Headmaster's study?

108

4   By the end of the story there can be little doubt as to who the school is being chosen for, the parents or the child. Read again lines 163 to the end, what are your views? Why, for instance, is the boy's face described as being 'haggard with anticipation'?

5   Either:
(a) When Charles is left alone with the boys they ask him a series of questions which he finds difficult to answer. The scene itself, however, is not directly described. Write it out as a brief playscript, showing the sort of questions and comments the boys would be likely to make.
Or:
(b) On returning home, Charles decides to write a letter to Simon Wilcox, where he describes, in some detail, his experiences of the day and goes on to ask Simon for his views of the school. Write out the letter which you feel Charles would write, and perhaps include Simon's reply.

Response

1   Write about a time when you have felt threatened or irritated by people who are obviously trying very hard to 'make the right impression'.

2   Appearances can be deceptive. Write about a place, a person or an incident, whose outward appearance turns out to be the complete opposite of its inner reality.

25

Five go mad in Dorset
by The Comic Strip

The children are seen cycling through the countryside. They stop on the brow of a hill overlooking rolling countryside and are having a picnic.

DICK   I say, this is a jolly wizard lunch, Anne. You're really going to make someone a great little wife one day.

JULIAN   Umm. My favourite. Ham and turkey sandwiches, heaps of tomatoes, fresh lettuce and lashings of ginger beer.

In the background two men, Rooky and Hunchy, are seen carrying a box across a field. They stop and start digging a pit.

ANNE   This is just the kind of holiday I like, picnicky meals and not too much adventure.

DICK   Well don't speak too soon, old thing.

A black car draws up. A black-gloved hand throws out a piece of meat.

MAN'S VOICE   Here, Fido.

He drives off at speed. Timmy, the dog, gobbles the meat.

GEORGE   That's strange. Why on earth would somebody want to feed Timmy?

JULIAN   Yes that was rather odd.

DICK   Ssh. I say look over there.

They notice the two men digging.

GEORGE   What a strange pair!

JULIAN   Yes one's got a big nose and thick lips and the other one's got mean, clever little eyes.

DICK   And they're unshaven. Just look how they're slouching.

ANNE   Urgh! Pooh! I hope they don't come near us. I feel as if I can smell them from here.

GEORGE   Ssh. I can hear them talking.

HUNCHY   What about the sparklers, Rooky?

ROOKY   Don't worry, Hunchy, I'll take care of that.

HUNCHY   Well now that you're out of gaol you'd better lie low.

GEORGE   D'you think they're escaped convicts?

DICK   Yes, or traitors to our country.

JULIAN   We'd better call the police.

ANNE   Oh look Timmy's fallen over.

Timmy is lying still in the grass.

GEORGE   Oh crikey, he's been poisoned!
JULIAN   Never mind, George, we'll get another. Come on
everybody let's find a telephone!

They cycle off. . . .

The five are all together again by Enid Blyton

'Phew!' said Julian, mopping his wet forehead. 'What a day! Let's go
and live at the Equator — it would be cool compared to this!'

He stood leaning on his bicycle, out of breath with a long steep
ride up a hill. Dick grinned at him. 'You're out of training, Ju!' he said.
5   'Let's sit down for a bit and look at the view. We're pretty high up!'

They leaned their bicycles against a nearby gate and sat down,
their backs against the lower bars. Below them spread the Dorset
countryside, shimmering in the heat of the day, the distance almost
lost in a blue haze. A small breeze came wandering round, and Julian
10   sighed in relief.

'I'd never have come on this biking trip if I'd guessed it was going
to be as hot as this!' he said. 'Good thing Anne didn't come — she'd
have given up the first day.'

'George wouldn't have minded,' said Dick. 'She's game enough
15   for anything.'

'Good old Georgina,' said Julian, shutting his eyes. 'I'll be glad
to see the girls again. Fun to be on our own, of course — but things
always seem to happen when the four of us are together.'

'*Five*, you mean,' said Dick, tipping his hat over his eyes. 'Don't
20   forget old Timmy. What a dog! Never knew one that had such a wet
lick as Tim. I say — won't it be fun to meet them all! Don't let's forget
the time, Julian. Hey, wake up, ass! If we go to sleep now, we'll not be
in time to meet the girls' bus.'

Julian was almost asleep. Dick looked at him and laughed. Then
25   he looked at his watch, and did a little calculating. It was half past two.

'Let's see now — Anne and George will be on the bus that stops
at Finniston Church at five past three,' he thought. 'Finniston is about
a mile away, down this hill. I'll give Julian fifteen minutes to have a
nap — and hope to goodness I don't fall asleep myself!'

The five are all together again

30 He felt his own eyes closing after a minute, and got up at once to walk about. The two girls and Tim *must* be met, because they would have suitcases with them, which the boys planned to wheel along on their bicycles.

The five were going to stay at a place called Finniston Farm, set
35 on a hill above the little village of Finniston. None of them had been there before, nor even heard of it. It had all come about because George's mother had heard from an old school friend, who had told her that she was taking paying guests at her farm-house — and had asked her to recommend visitors to her. George had promptly said
40 she would like to go there with her cousins in the summer holidays.

'Hope it's a decent place!' thought Dick, gazing down into the valley, where corn-fields waved in the little breeze. 'Anyway, we shall only be there for two weeks — and it *will* be fun to be together again.'

He looked at his watch. Time to go! He gave Julian a push. 'Hey
45 — wake up!'

''Nother ten minutes,' muttered Julian, trying to turn over, as if he were in bed. He rolled against the gate-bars and fell on to the hard dry earth below. He sat up in surprise. 'Gosh — I thought I was in bed!' he said. 'My word, I could have gone on sleeping for hours.'
50 'Well, it's time to go and meet the bus,' said Dick. 'I've had to walk about all the time you were asleep, I was so afraid I'd go off myself. Come on, Julian — we really must go!'

They rode down the hill, going cautiously round the sharp corners, remembering how many times they had met herds of cows,
55 wide farm-carts, tractors and the like, on their way through this great farming county. Ah — there was the village, at the bottom of the hill. It looked old and peaceful and half-asleep.

'Thank goodness it sells ginger-beer and ice-creams!' said Dick, seeing a small shop with a big sign in the window. 'I feel as if I want to
60 hang out my tongue, like Timmy does, I'm so thirsty!'

'Let's find the church and the bus-stop,' said Julian. 'I saw a spire as we rode down the hill, but it disappeared when we got near the bottom.'

'There's the bus!' said Dick, as he heard the noise of wheels
65 rumbling along in the distance. 'Look, here it comes. We'll follow it.'

'There's Anne in it — and George, look!' shouted Julian. 'We're here exactly on time! Whoo-hoo, George!'

The bus came to a stop by the old church, and out jumped Anne and George, each with a suitcase — and out leapt old Timmy too, his
70 tongue hanging down, very glad to be out of the hot, jerky, smelly bus.

'There are the boys!' shouted George, and waved wildly as the bus went off again. 'Julian! Dick! I'm so glad you're here to meet us!'

The two boys rode up, and jumped off their bikes, while Timmy

leapt round them, barking madly. They thumped the girls on their
backs, and grinned at them. 'Just the same old sixpences!' said Dick.
'You've got a spot on your chin, George, and why on *earth* have you
tied your hair into a pony-tail, Anne?'

'You're not very polite, Dick,' said George, bumping him with
her suitcase. 'I can't think why Anne and I looked forward so much to
seeing you again. Here, take my suitcase — haven't you any
manners?'

'Plenty,' said Dick, and grabbed the case. 'I just can't get over
Anne's new hair-do. I don't like it, Anne — do you, Ju? Pony-tail! A
donkey-tail would suit you better, Anne!'

'It's all right — it's just because the back of my neck was so hot,'
said Anne, shaking her hair free in a hurry. She hated her brothers to
find fault with her. Julian gave her arm a squeeze.

'Nice to see you both,' he said. 'What about some ginger-beer
and ice-cream? There's a shop over there that sells them. And I've a
sudden longing for nice juicy plums!'

'You haven't said a *word* to Timmy yet,' said George, half-
offended. 'He's been trotting round you and licking your hands —
and he's so dreadfully hot and thirsty!'

'Shake paws, Tim,' said Dick, and Timmy politely put up his
right paw. He shook hands with Julian too and then promptly went
mad, careering about and almost knocking over a small boy on a
bicycle.

'Come on, Tim — want an ice-cream?' said Dick, laying his hand
on the big dog's head. 'Hark at him panting, George — I bet he
wishes he could unzip his hairy coat and take it off! Don't you, Tim?'

'Woof!' said Tim, and slapped his tail against Dick's bare legs.

They all trooped into the ice-cream shop. It was half dairy, half
baker's. A small girl of about ten came to serve them.

'Mum's lying down,' she said. 'What can I get you? Ice-creams, I
suppose? That's what everyone wants today.'

'You supposed right,' said Julian. 'A large one each, please —
five in all — and four bottles of ginger pop as well.'

'*Five* ice-creams — do you want one for that dog, then?' said the
girl in surprise, looking at Timmy.

'Woof,' he said at once.

'There you are,' said Dick, 'he said yes!'

Soon the Five were eating their cold ice-creams, Timmy licking
his from a saucer. Before he had had many licks, the ice-cream slid
from the saucer, and Timmy chased it all the way round the shop, as it
slid away from his vigorous licks. The little girl watched him,
fascinated.

'I must apologize for his manners,' said Julian, solemnly. 'He
hasn't been very well brought up.' He at once had a glare from

The five are all together again

120 George, and grinned. He opened his bottle of ginger-beer. 'Nice and cold,' he said. 'Here's a happy fortnight to us all!' He drank half the glass at top speed, and set it down with a great sigh.

'Well, blessings on the person who invented ice-cream, ginger-pop and the rest!' he said. 'I'd rather invent things like that any day

125 than rockets and bombs. Ha — I feel better now. What about you others? Do you feel like going to find the farm?'

'Whose farm?' asked the little girl, coming out from behind the counter to pick up Timmy's saucer. Timmy gave her a large, wet and loving lick as she bent down.

130 'Ooooh!' she said, pushing him away. 'He licked all down my face!'

'Probably thought you were an ice-cream,' said Dick, giving her his hanky to wipe her cheek. 'The farm we want is called Finniston Farm. Do you know it?'

135 'Oh *yes*,' said the little girl. 'You go down the village street, right to the end, and turn up the lane there — up to the right. The farmhouse is at the top of the lane. Are you staying with the Philpots?'

'Yes. Do you know them?' asked Julian, getting out some money to pay the bill.

140 'I know the twins there,' said the girl. 'The two Harries. At least, I don't know them *well*— nobody does. They're just wrapped up in each other, they never make any friends. You look out for their old Great-Grand-dad— *he's* a one, he is! He once fought a mad bull and knocked it out! And his *voice*— you can hear it for miles! I was real

145 scared of going near the farm when I was little. But Mrs Philpot, she's nice. You'll like her. The twins are very good to her — and to their Dad, too — work like farm-hands all the holidays. You won't know t'other from which, they're so alike!'

'Why did you call them the two Harries?' asked Anne, curiously.

150 'Oh, because they've both . . .' began the child, and then broke off as a plump woman came bustling into the shop.

'Janie — you go and see to the baby for me — I'll see to the shop now. Run along!'

Away went the small girl, scuttling through the door.

155 'Little gasbag she is!' said her mother. 'Anything more you want?'

'No thanks,' said Julian, getting up. 'We must go. We're to stay at Finniston Farm, so we may be seeing you again soon. We liked the ice-creams!'

160 'Oh — so you're going there, are you?' said the plump woman. 'I wonder how you'll get on with the Harries! And keep out of Grand-dad's way — he's over eighty, but he can still give a mighty good thumping to anyone who crosses him!'

114

The Five went out into the hot sun again. Julian grinned round at
165 the others. 'Well — shall we go and find the nice Mrs Philpot — the
unfriendly Harries, whoever they are — and the fearsome Great-
Grand-dad? Sounds an interesting household, doesn't it?'

From *The Five on Finniston Farm* by Enid Blyton

Understanding

1   Read again lines 1–52 from *Five on Finniston Farm*. Who, in
your opinion, is the 'leader' between Julian and Dick and
what sort of 'leadership qualities' does he show? List as
many as you can find.

2   Re-read lines 74–91. How would you describe Dick's
behaviour towards Anne and George? In what ways does
Julian's behaviour differ?

3   Watch out for the Philpots! But why exactly? What clues are
you given which suggest they may be just a little bit odd?

4   Now turn back to the 'Five Go Mad' extract. How are the two
men Rooky and Hunchy made to seem so threatening and
extraordinary? List as many writer's tricks as you can find.

5   Either:
(a) Continue the second story, in true Enid Blyton fashion, to
include the first meetings with the nice Mrs Philpot, the
unfriendly Harries and the fearsome Great-Grand-dad!
Or:
(b) Return to the Comic Strip playscript version and
continue the adventure here. Not forgetting the lashings of
ginger beer!

Response

1   Is it possible to bring the 'famous five' up-to-date? Invent
some suitable characters that might represent four, present
day school students (and their dog). How would they differ
from the original five? Would the girls behave in the same
way? Would the boys, for that matter? What new phrases
might they use? How would they relax and what sort of
adventures would they have? Try out some possibilities
either as a story or as a playscript.

26

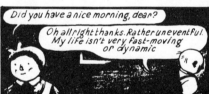

by Raymond Briggs (one)

When The Wind Blows tells the tragic, yet also comic, story of Jim and Hilda Bloggs' attempt to survive the effects of a nuclear attack with the help of an official Home Office booklet *Protect and Survive*. The play ends with their slide towards inevitable death due to radiation poisoning.

Understanding

1   The first five frames of the strip show Jim walking home alone through the countryside. Why do you think the artist (Raymond Briggs) chose to begin the book in this way?

2   Frames 6–12 introduce the reader to the couple, their home and their general way of life. What have you discovered so far about Jim and Hilda, especially the way they talk and behave to each other? In what ways are they similar? In what ways are they different?

3   The next five frames (13–17) contain a whole series of confusions and muddles from both Jim and Hilda. Firstly, list as many confusions as you can find in these frames. Then explain why you think Raymond Briggs wanted to stress these muddles at this stage? What might his reasons be?

4   Frame 18 concludes the first page of the book. Examine the frame closely, both picture and speech. Then describe your thoughts and feelings as you explore the contrast between what Jim is saying in this frame and how he appears to you visually? What sense can you make of his expression and stance, especially in the light of what he has just said to his wife?

by Raymond Briggs (two)

Jim and Hilda Bloggs' country cottage and garden in South-East England. An early morning in Spring.

The cottage is very neat and well looked-after. Everything inside is clean, tidy and polished. The small kitchen is spotless. The garden presents a very pleasant — even idyllic — scene. Sunlight, bird song, cottage garden flowers (hollyhocks and nasturtiums), a bird bath, home-made garden seat painted green, neat rows of vegetables and a little shed.

As the Curtain *rises we hear the distant sound of cattle, sheep, church clock, together with the occasional train, car, motorcycle and tractor, to contrast with the total silence after the Bomb.*

Jim and Hilda Bloggs are a working-class couple in their mid to late sixties, newly retired from London. Hilda is making tea and bustling about in the kitchen. The radio is playing music quietly — Radio Two. Jim is pottering about the garden, weeding and humming to himself.

Jim (*gazing up at the sky*) Lovely day, dear. Nice breeze.
Hilda (*clattering in the kitchen*) The forecast says rain. Showers before evening.
Jim I don't suppose it'll be much. (*He sucks his finger and holds it up knowledgeably*) The wind's in the east.
Hilda Kettle's boiling, James.

The Paper Boy, on a bicycle, arrives with a bell ring and a skid and hands Jim the paper over the hedge.

Paper Boy Morning, Mr Bloggs.
Jim Morning, Tom. Thanks.

The Paper Boy races off with another gravelly swerve and skid.

Mind how you go! (*He takes out his spectacles.*) You'll get yourself killed! (*He opens the paper, reads the front page and goes very still. He then sits down heavily on the garden seat, still staring at the paper.*)

Hilda James! Tea's made!

Jim is oblivious, lost in the paper.

James! I won't tell you again. Your tea is ready.

Jim gradually pulls himself together and slowly goes indoors. He walks like someone stunned.

Whatever is the matter with you, James? You look as if you've seen a ghost.

Jim Just been reading the paper.

Hilda Oh, that thing! I never look at it — except The Stars.

Jim sits down heavily again, ignoring the tea.

Jim (*absently*) We must keep abreast of the International Situation, ducks. The decisions made by the Powers That Be will get to us in the end.

Hilda Politics and sport, that's all there is in it.

Jim picks up the paper again and stares at it.

Jim They say there may be a Pre-Emptive Strike, dear.

Hilda Oh not another strike! It's wicked. I'd have them all locked up. Blessed Communists!

Jim It's not that sort of strike, ducks. (*Pause*) It all looks pretty humpty.

Hilda (*from the kitchen*) Sausages or egg, dear?

Jim Egg, thanks. It looks as if the Balloon could go up at any moment.

Hilda What balloon, dear? Fried or boiled?

Jim Boiled, thanks. Oh, I don't know . . . The Balloon . . . or is it the Maroon? I can't remember.

Hilda What *are* you talking about, James?

Jim It looks as if there's going to be a War, dear.

Understanding

1   The playscript begins very differently to the comic book. Carefully re-read the opening stage notes and the first five lines of script. In what ways has your understanding of this couple changed since the comic book version? There are some factual differences. List and comment on these but concentrate on the picture you have created of this couple in your mind's eye and the ways in which this has changed or developed?

2   The incident with the paper boy is unique to the play. Why do you think Raymond Briggs has included it here? What sense do you make of Jim's comment as the boy races off?

3   From what you have read of the two versions, say which involved you more as a reader, the playscript or the cartoon strip? Which version would you prefer to continue reading? Give as many reasons as you can for your answer.

Response

1   You may know that a feature length cartoon film has been made of *When The Wind Blows*. When it was first released *The Times* printed the following article.

Teachers risk being sued over cartoon
By Sheila Gunn
Political Staff

Teachers run the risk of being sued by parents if they show the cartoon film, *When the Wind Blows*, which portrays the slow death of an elderly couple after a nuclear attack on Britain.

The Department of Education and Science yesterday gave a warning that unless the showing was part of a balanced discussion on the use of nuclear weapons then schools would be in breach of the new Education Act.

'The onus is on schools to prove that they provided a balanced opinion on this issue.'

The film, now showing at cinemas, is based on Raymond Briggs's book telling the tragi-comic story of Jim and Hilda Bloggs's attempt to survive the effects of a nuclear attack with the help of the Home Office booklet, *Protect and Survive*.

Lord Jenkins of Putney, the former Labour arts minister, asked the Government for an assurance that it would not prevent a showing of the film in schools or elsewhere.

Lady Hooper, for the Government, replied: 'The showing of this film in schools or elsewhere will be subject to the relevant statutory provisions.'

A clause was added to the Education Bill last year aimed at banning politically biased teaching in schools.

It was later redrafted and now states that the school authorities '. . . shall take such steps as are reasonably practicable to secure that where political issues are brought to the attention of pupils while they are at the school or taking part in ex-curriculum activities . . . they are offered a balanced presentation of opposing views'.

It has been in effect since January 7.

The DES confirmed yesterday that the wording would cover both a screening at school or a school party going to the cinema. The school would be safe from prosecution if it could prove the showing was balanced.

How do you react to these statements? From what you have read so far, would you consider *When The Wind Blows* to be politically biased and therefore in need of being 'balanced' by the appropriate 'presentation of opposing views'?

2   **However, Bel Mooney, a journalist writing in *Sanity Magazine*, commented: 'It is a book and film I would certainly like children to read and see. We underestimate our children all the time: their ability to understand, their perception of what is right or wrong, their resilience, their imagination.'**

    Write a detailed reply, either to the Department of Education and Science (DES) or to Bel Mooney, arguing for your point of view on the suitability of *When The Wind Blows*.

27

THE FOREST ON THE SUPER HIGHWAY
by Italo Calvino

Cold has a thousand shapes and a thousand ways of moving in the world: on the sea it gallops like a troop of horses, on the countryside it falls like a swarm of locusts, in the cities like a knife-blade it slashes the streets and penetrates the chinks of unheated houses. In
5 Marcovaldo's house that evening they had burned the last kindling, and the family, all bundled in overcoats, was watching the embers fade in the stove, and the little clouds rise from their own mouths at every breath. They had stopped talking; the little clouds spoke for them: the wife emitted great long ones like sighs, the children puffed
10 them out like assorted soap-bubbles, and Marcovaldo blew them upwards in jerks, like flashes of genius that promptly vanish.

In the end Marcovaldo made up his mind: 'I'm going to look for wood; who knows? I might find some.' He stuffed four or five newspapers between his shirt and his jacket as breastplates against
15 gusts of air, he hid a long, snaggle-tooth saw under his overcoat, and thus he went out into the night, followed by the long, hopeful looks of his family. He made a papery rustle at every step, the saw peeped out now and then above his collar.

Looking for wood in the city: easier said than done! Marcovaldo
20 headed at once towards a little patch of public park that stood between two streets. All was deserted. Marcovaldo studied the naked trees, one by one, thinking of his family, waiting for him with their teeth chattering.

Little Michelino, his teeth chattering, was reading a book of
25 fairy-tales, borrowed from the small library at school. The book told of a child, son of a woodsman, who went out with a hatchet to chop wood in the forest. 'That's the place to go!' Michelino said, 'the forest! There's wood there, all right!' Born and raised in the city, he had never seen a forest, not even at a distance.

30 Then and there, he worked it out with his brothers: one took a hatchet, one a hook, one a rope; they said goodbye to their Mamma and went out in search of a forest.

They walked around the city, illuminated by street-lamps, and they saw only houses: not a sign of a forest. They encountered an
35 occasional passer-by, but they didn't dare ask him where a forest was. And so they reached the area where the houses of the city ended and the street turned into a highway.

At the sides of the highway, the children saw the forest: a thick
growth of strange trees blocked the view of the plain. Their trunks
40   were very very slender, erect or slanting; and their crowns were flat
and outspread, revealing the strangest shapes and the strangest
colours when a passing car illuminated them with its headlights.
Boughs in the form of a toothpaste tube, a face, cheese, hand, razor,
bottle, cow, tyre, all dotted with a foliage of letters of the alphabet.
45   'Hurrah!' Michelino said, 'this is the forest!'
And, spellbound, the brothers watched the moon rise among
those strange shadows: 'How beautiful it is . . .'
Michelino immediately reminded them of their purpose in
coming there: wood. So they chopped down a little tree in the form of
50   a yellow primrose blossom, cut it into bits, and took it home.
Marcovaldo came home with his scant armful of damp bran-
ches, and found the stove burning.
'Where did you find it?' he cried, pointing to what remained of the
billboard, which, being of plywood, had burned very quickly.
55   'In the forest!' the children said.
'What forest?'
'The one by the highway. It's full of wood!'
Since it was so simple, and there was need of more wood, he
thought he might as well follow the children's example, and
60   Marcovaldo again went out with his saw. He went to the highway.
Officer Astolfo, of the highway police, was a bit short-sighted,
and on night duty, racing on his motorcycle, he should have worn
eyeglasses; but he didn't say so, for fear it would block his
advancement.
65   That evening, there was a report that on the superhighway, a
bunch of kids was knocking down billboards. Officer Astolfo set out to
inspect.
On either side of the road, the forest of strange figures,
admonishing and gesticulating, accompanied Astolfo, who peered at
70   them one by one, widening his near-sighted eyes. There, in the beam
of his motorcycle's headlight, he caught a little urchin who had
climbed up on a billboard. Astolfo put on the brakes: 'Hey, what are
you doing there? Jump down this minute!' The kid didn't move and
stuck out its tongue. Astolfo approached and saw it was an ad for
75   processed cheese, with a big child licking his lips. 'Yes, of course,'
Astolfo said, and zoomed off.
A little later, in the shadow of a huge billboard, he illuminated a
sad, frightened face. 'Don't make a move! Don't try running away!'
But nobody ran away: it was a suffering human face painted in the
80   midst of a foot covered with corns: an ad for a corn-remover. 'Oh,
sorry,' Astolfo said, and dashed away.

THE FOREST ON THE SUPER HIGHWAY

The billboard for a headache tablet was a gigantic head of a man, his hands over his eyes, in pain. Astolfo sped past, and the headlight illuminated Marcovaldo, who had scrambled to the top
85 with his saw, trying to cut off a slice. Dazzled by the light, Marcovaldo huddled down and remained motionless, clinging to an ear of the big head, where the saw had already reached the middle of the brow.

Astolfo examined it carefully and said: 'Oh, yes. Stappa tablets! Very effective ad! Smart idea! That little man up there with the saw
90 represents the migraine that is cutting the head in two. I got it right away!' And he went off, content.

All was silence and cold. Marcovaldo heaved a sigh of relief, settled on his uncomfortable perch, and resumed work. The muffled scrape of the saw against the wood spread through the moonlit sky.

Understanding

1   After reading the first paragraph (lines 1–11), why do you think it was so cold in Marcovaldo's house on this particular evening?

2   Line 19 reads: 'Looking for wood in the city: easier said than done!' As a reader, how prepared were you for this information? Had you pictured the story until then, as being set in a city? If not, where had you placed Marcovaldo and his family? What were your reasons for this placing? List as many as you can.

3   When the children went out to search for wood they eventually reached the area 'where the houses of the city ended and the street turned into a highway' (lines 36–37). The next seven lines (until line 44) describe what they thought to be a forest. When you read those lines for the first time, what were your thoughts as the 'strange trees' were being described?

4   Lines 68–76 describe Officer Astolfo's reactions to the first billboard. Can you explain the policeman's confusion here? Why does he behave in this way?

5　　The final billboard incident (lines 82–91) provides the biggest confusion of them all. What exactly is happening here? Write down the thoughts that would be running through the mind of Marcovaldo as the police officer approached the billboard.

6　　Things are not always what they seem. Can you see any similarities in the kinds of mistakes made by the young children earlier in the story and the mistakes made by Officer Astolfo towards the end? Does this comparison tell you anything about the difficulties of living in the modern world?

Response

1　　Write about a time when you have fundamentally misunderstood something or someone and, as a result, ended up looking a bit of a fool!

2　　There are times when events from real life come very close to resembling scenes from traditional folk tales and stories. Choose a theme from a story you know well and re-write it as it could possibly occur in the very different circumstances of your own time, place and customs.

28

REMOTE HOUSE

by Hans Magnus Enzensberger

This passage is from a book called Poems for People Who Don't Read
Poems.

> when i wake up
> the house is silent.
> only the birds make noise.
> through the window i see
> no one. here
> no road passes.
> there is no wire in the sky
> and no wire in the earth.
> quiet the living things lie
> under the axe.
>
> i put my water on to boil.
> i cut my bread.
> unquiet i press
> the red push-button
> of the small transistor.
>
> 'caribbean crisis . . . washes whiter
> and whiter and whiter . . . troops ready to fly out . . .
> phase three . . . that's the way i love you . . .
> amalgamated steel stocks are back to par . . .'
>
> i do not take the axe.
> i do not smash the gadget to pieces.
> the voice of terror
> calms me; it says:
> we are still alive.
>
> the house is silent.
> i do not know how to set traps
> or make an axe out of flint,
> when the last blade
> has rusted.

REMOTE HOUSE

Understanding

1   Try to make sense of this poem by reducing it to its barest essentials. Firstly, eliminate any unnecessary lines until you have a maximum of 20 lines remaining. Which lines would go first? Then reduce the poem down to a maximum of 10 lines, and finally to 5 lines (one line from each verse?). Try to give reasons for your deletions and final selection.

2   Suggest a separate title for each of the poem's five verses.

3   Consider the possible background to this poem. Write down who the 'speaker' might be, where and when the poem is set and what exactly is happening, in your opinion.

4   Imagine yourself as a visitor to this 'remote house'. Write out a possible conversation you might have with the 'speaker' in this poem. If the idea works, develop it into a script for a short radio play.

Response

1   The collection from which this poem was chosen is called *Poems for People Who Don't Read Poems*. With this thought in mind, write a poem of your own which would suit such a collection.

29

GOLDEN GIRLS

Louise Page

The play extract which follows concerns a women's 4×100 metres, sprint relay team. They are about to begin a series of major tournaments leading up to the European Championships. Their chances of success are good but the stakes are high. Laces is their trainer, Vivien is the team doctor and Hilary represents a large pharmaceutical company interested in sponsoring the team.

Scene One

HILARY Laces, I must get on, I have to be back in London tonight.

LACES Okay girls —

Silence.

Hilary —

HILARY I'd like to spend a few minutes with you on the do's and don'ts of being in the Golden Girls squad. We don't believe that sponsors should interfere with their er — there's not really a word for it — those we're sponsoring. But if you work for any organisation there are a few ground rules. I've brought with me several crates of Golden Girls shampoo and from now on I'd ask you only to use Golden Girls. I've brought up your tracksuits and running togs. I know yellow doesn't suit everybody —

SUE I look dreadful in yellow.

HILARY But I think our designers have managed to find a shade that will do justice to all of you. We're keen for you to wear these at all times. I know that some of you have certain affinities to various articles of clothing but I hope you'll be able to re-invest those in the Golden Girls kit.

No one wants to lay down rules of behaviour to

grown-women but I think you must all realize that being a golden girl has certain responsibilities. Obviously we want winners but if you don't win, don't forget the glory there is to be obtained by being a good loser. The joy of the race is in the running, after all. I think we'd all agree that we wouldn't look up to a heroine who swears like a trooper, even if she has just lost. I needn't stress how important it is for you to stress that you are sponsored by us. That as athletes you are assisted by us for the money that allows you to compete and a little that we put into your trust funds but nothing more. No one wants to hear the dirty rustle of five pound notes.

PAULINE   I wouldn't mind, however dirty.

Hilary allows herself to laugh.

HILARY   Have I missed out anything Laces?

LACES   Sounds fine to me.

HILARY   One more thing. Any trouble, any sort of suspension or ban and we'll drop you like a hot potato.

DORCAS   Can we drop you if you do something we don't like?

HILARY   What could we possibly do?

SUE   Don't you test shampoo on the eyes of rabbits, things like that?

HILARY   The last thing I want to say is you'll find it difficult in interviews — people will do everything they can to avoid you mentioning the name of the product. But the more accidental slips you make the more you help our sales and consequently what we can invest in you. It can become a little game. We're going to reward you with an extra £100 in your trust funds everytime you manage to mention Ortolan or Golden Girls. Most of all I want you to enjoy the benefits that Ortolan sponsorship can give you and to put everything you can towards first Gateshead and Crystal Palace and then triumphing in Athens. Do that and we'll see where we can go from there.

Silence.

JANET   Thank you

HILARY   Laces —

LACES   I want you all warmed up on the track in 20 minutes.

They leave.

GOLDEN GIRLS

Scene Two

Cut to music for ad.

NUTBROWN

VOICE	Golden Girls, puts you ahead in the race. *Music.*
HILARY	That's it. Your whole thirty seconds worth.
VIVIEN	It's very good. Not that I know anything about adverts of course.
HILARY	We've booked every slot for it during Gateshead.
VIVIEN	Be impossible for anyone not to get the message.
HILARY	We're taking a gamble. We could look very silly.
VIVIEN	You've got a lot staked on them haven't you?
HILARY	Yes.
VIVIEN	There are a lot of things affect results.
HILARY	You're the doctor, you should know.
VIVIEN	It goes beyond the physical. There's a mental attitude as well.
HILARY	You and I wouldn't be where we are if we couldn't deal with that. Why did you run?
VIVIEN	Pleasure.
HILARY	I find it quite extraordinary.
VIVIEN	Wanting to be good at something? You understand ambition.
HILARY	So what do you get out of it now?
VIVIEN	Being team doctor.
	Pause.
	The chance to do some pure research. There's a chair in medical psychology coming up in about three years time that I'd like to go for.
HILARY	Is that enough time to make a reputation?
VIVIEN	I was a distance runner. I know a lot about timing my run from the back.
HILARY	More wine?
VIVIEN	Please.
	Sound effect of wine being poured.
HILARY	I want golden girls.
VIVIEN	I'll give them to you.
	They chink glasses– music –

cut to Vivien's office.

Scene Three

VIVIEN *Entering.*

Sorry I'm late.

She puts down a case with papers on her desk — opens it.

LACES I managed to amuse myself.

VIVIEN Those files are supposed to be private and confidential.

LACES You've got a lot of information on them. Their ups, their downs.

VIVIEN No stone left unturned in the pursuit of excellence. There's something I want to try. Don't look suspicious before you've heard me out.

She sits.

LACES It's something you don't think I'm going to like.

VIVIEN Just hear me out.

LACES If it's not legitimate I don't want to know.

VIVIEN It wouldn't show up in urine tests. Or blood tests or anywhere.

LACES So it's not a drug?

VIVIEN A drug that no one would ever be able to prove.

LACES It's not ethical.

VIVIEN You'd have no objection to them training at altitude?

LACES No.

VIVIEN A lot of countries couldn't afford to do that. Ethics? You can't be a purist. Sport isn't like that any more.

LACES There isn't anything safe.

VIVIEN This is.

LACES And legitimate?

VIVIEN Yes.

LACES Pull the other one.

VIVIEN Hydromel.

LACES It's a drug and it's not legitimate.

VIVIEN Not if they aren't really taking it.

LACES A placebo?

VIVIEN   Exactly. There's a pill called Similexon. It's made from sugar and cornstarch. The stuff turkish delight is rolled in. They'd get through every dope test going.

LACES   Then how come they run faster?

VIVIEN   They'll believe they can because they'll think they're taking Hydromel.

LACES   You're going to tell them that's what it is?

VIVIEN   I'll certainly hint that that's what it is. They'll draw their own conclusions.

LACES   You'll never convince them.

VIVIEN   Won't I?

LACES   If they think it's any sort of drug they'll have scruples.

VIVIEN   Well Dorcas doesn't have them for a start.

LACES   She's asked?

VIVIEN   Questions about other teams. What are they on? Where do they get it? Why aren't they found out?

LACES   That is not asking.

VIVIEN   If other athletes are prepared to take something —

LACES   It doesn't mean mine are.

VIVIEN   Not if they thought it put them on an equal footing? A fighting chance? If I convince them it's absolutely undetectable?

LACES   You're not convincing me.

VIVIEN   See this?

LACES   Urine analysis.

VIVIEN   Of my urine after taking Similexon. And because it's a placebo, not a drug, there is nothing to find.
Pause.

LACES   And they still run faster?

VIVIEN   Precisely. If they believe it's Hydromel it becomes a case of mind over matter. Psychologically they just might find themselves those precious hundreths of a second. Think of the future it would give them.

LACES   If it was found?

VIVIEN   There will be nothing to find. I'm a doctor, trust me.

Understanding

1   In her 2nd and 3rd speeches of Scene One Hilary outlines a 'few ground rules' which are linked to the sponsorship deal. Using your own words, write out those ground rules as you understand them.

2   Towards the end of Hilary's introductory remarks, Dorcas, a member of the relay team, asks a question. How is this handled by Hilary? What might be her reasons for acting in the way she does to this question?

3   Hilary's final point to the team can be found in her 7th speech. What are your views on this sponsorship? Is it just a normal part of any commercial deal? Or is it asking too much of the girls, over and above their athletic talents? Where do you stand?

4   Vivien's conversation with Hilary during Scene Two is interesting for the light it sheds on Vivien as a character. Referring closely to the evidence contained in this scene, how would you describe Vivien? What sort of person is she? Give your reasons.

5   Vivien's plan becomes clear during Scene Three as she gradually explains her intentions to Laces (the team coach). Laces' reaction is confused. At the start she seems to be against the idea, but by the end — who knows? Imagine that you are Laces an hour or so after the conversation with Vivien. You are trying to make up your mind how to respond to the doctor. Should you cooperate or refuse? To help you decide you make two lists: one with all the points in favour of cooperating; the other, in favour of refusal. Think back over Vivien's argument. What would you list in each column?

Response

1   Write about a time when you have been tempted to 'bend the rules' in order to achieve something you really wanted. What conflicting thoughts ran through your mind?

2   Commercial sponsorship may well be an attractive solution to many hard pressed sports enthusiasts. But are there hidden costs? Choose an example you are familiar with, weigh up the arguments for and against, and then go on to decide how you could best highlight this dilemma by writing a short story or playscript built around just such a debate. *Golden Girls* managed it — now over to you!

just visiting

by Dee Philips

Alan pushed open the door of the small terraced house, remembering not to knock. There was no front garden, and he stepped straight from the pavement into the tiny hall, then across to the front room where the double bed had been put up. It filled most of the space,
5 leaving just enough beside it for a kitchen chair where old Mrs Bennett, a neighbour, sat knitting, turning at the rustle of his anorak.

'There's a good boy,' she whispered, getting up stiffly and pushing her needles into a paper bag. 'I thought you'd come today. District Nurse has been and gone.' Then, even more softly, 'Did your
10 mother say anything about looking in?'

He did not know what to say, and shrugged his shoulders. She clicked her tongue and rummaged in her handbag, producing two toffees which she handed to him.

'Never mind. You sit with your gran for a bit while I run over and
15 see how Maureen's placed,' she said. 'She'll come in for an hour or so, and let you get off to school.'

Alan took off his anorak and held it for a moment, then let it fall to the floor, as there was nowhere to put it but the bed, which seemed wrong. Then he sat down holding the toffees as the front door latch
20 clicked behind Mrs Bennett.

He had not looked at his grandmother till now, almost as if she were not there. And even when he looked he could not quite believe in her. Her hands lay out on top of the covers, twitching a little now and then, but apart from that she was very still, her face grey and sunk
25 in without her teeth, her nose looking outlandishly big and pointed, her eyes closed. As a rule the lively eyes held his attention, so that he had never noticed the signs of age upon her, and it seemed now as if the skin had wrinkled because there was no one inside.

He had guessed they would need him to stay today, and that it
30 would be different from the other visits. Last week, before things got really bad, there had been several people there when he went in one day after school. They were drinking her Wincarnis, almost like a party round her bed. 'Here's my old mate!' she had called out, and he flushed with embarrassment as they all turned to look at him. Then
35 after he kissed her she had begun to cry a little, saying he deserved better than he'd got, and something else in a whisper to Auntie Joyce, so that he had known they were talking about his mother.

It was quiet now, except for the loud tick of the clock on the mantelpiece, and he was glad of its regularity, suggesting something
40 that would go on for ever. He unwrapped one of the toffees and tried to pay attention to the ticks, counting and saying rhymes in his head to their rhythm, so that he need not think about what was happening on the bed:

January brings the snow,
45 Makes our feet and fingers glow,
February brings the rain,
Thaws the frozen lake again.
March brings breezes loud and shrill . . .

The worst thing about it was not knowing if she knew. Two days
50 ago Mrs Bennett had said, 'I reckon she knows everything that's going on, only she's saying nothing.' He hoped it wasn't true. To know you were nearly dead must be the worst thing you could ever know. You'd be yelling out, terrified, surely anyone would. But she lay so calm it didn't seem as if she had guessed.
55 He hoped that when his time came he would be shot. He had seen it on films and it was not too bad, certainly the best of the ways he had heard about. Immediately after the bang you would rise up on your toes, lean over backwards a bit, then drop, dead as a stone. It was better than this. But, at his age, he comforted himself, he had a
60 long way to go, with people inventing things all the time; it might never have to happen.
He did not feel at home in this room — had seldom been in it before — though Gran had let him look in at the things on the mantelpiece. The mantelpiece itself had a fringe of dark red cloth with
65 bobbles on the bottom, and as well as the clock there were two ornaments. One was a bridge with three little elephants crossing it, each smaller than the one in front. The other was a square china pot shaped like a cottage, with an Armistice poppy stuck through the chimney pot.
70 In normal times he came to Gran's most Saturdays when he had to look after Kevin. They would sit in the kitchen and have their best dinner of the week, with a pudding cooked in a basin. Kevin would prattle and bang his spoon and make them laugh, but Alan did not say much himself. When Gran asked him what it was like at the
75 Secondary he would tell her, but he did not often think of things to say if she did not ask. Gran talked all the time, saying what she was doing. 'There,' she'd say as she lit the gas. 'There's the kettle done — now, we'll just get the cups, one for you, one for me, and a little one for his lordship — that's the way.' She laughed a lot and sang softly,
80 and he always felt happy with her.

just visiting

April brings the primrose sweet,
Scatters daisies at our feet . . .

He unwrapped the second toffee; then, just as he had it halfway
to his mouth, froze, as he became aware that the old woman on the
85 bed was awake and watching him, her sharp black eyes staring
straight into his own, frowning and questioning. He said, 'Hello,
Gran,' but his voice sounded shaky and silly.

She began to move her lips, soundlessly at first, then all at once
the words burst through faintly, as if she had something in the way in
90 her throat. 'Tell 'em,' she whispered. 'Why don't you tell 'em to hurry
up! Bloody fool! Bloody pig-headed fool!'

Alan felt his hands clench in sudden fear, then the burning in his
eyes of tears he did not want. Her hands were picking at the covers
and she moved her head from side to side in distress. He did not
95 know what to do, but leaned forward now that she was mumbling
again, to catch the names she kept repeating: 'Sheila, Joyce, Sophie.
Hurry 'em up,' she begged. 'Tell 'em it's the second bell.'

She was trying to lift her head, twisting her mouth about, and he
guessed through his terror that she was living the old times, getting
100 her girls off to school in the days she often told him about. The old
face was taut with anxiety, and suddenly he leaned a little nearer, his
mouth close to hers, and said almost desperately, 'It's a holiday. They
haven't got to go today.'

She twisted her head right round to look directly at him again.
105 ''Oliday! What 'oliday?' she snapped.

He knew she did not recognise him and it made him feel braver,
so that he could invent almost anything to say to her, like talking to a
stranger he would never see again; and he went on speaking softly,
looking into her face:
110 'It's half-term, Gran; no one's got to go nowhere. We can stay
indoors, it's all right.' He tucked the covers around her shoulders.
'You can have a lie-in,' he said almost cheerfully.

For a moment the old woman's face relaxed and she stopped
moving her head about and lay still, looking at him. 'Somebody'd
115 better tell 'em, then,' she said, and he answered her confidently now,
'I've told 'em; everything's done. Go to sleep again, it's all right.'

She closed her eyes and he leaned back in the kitchen chair,
frightened at the pounding of his heart. His face was flushed and hot,
but there was a glad feeling at the back of his mind that he had done it
120 right.

136

Understanding

1   From the evidence of the first seven lines, how would you describe the style of life Alan's Gran was used to? Give reasons for your answer.

2   Alan's mother is mentioned on two occasions. What impression do you have of her from what is said and hinted at? Again, give your reasons.

3   Line 59 originally contained Alan's age in years and months. From all you have read, how old would you estimate Alan to be? What evidence is there for your decision?

4   Line 70 mentions the 'normal times' when Alan would visit Gran with Kevin and have their 'best dinner of the week'. What would be so special about these visits? Mention as many things as you can.

5   The extract ends with the words 'there was a glad feeling at the back of his mind that he had done it right.' Explain in your own words what Alan has 'done right'. Why do you think he was so pleased with himself?

6   Either:
(a) On leaving Alan, Mrs Bennett calls on Maureen to see if she could relieve the boy and allow him to get off to school. They stand talking for a while, discussing the grandmother, Alan and his mother. Write down the conversation they would have.
Or:
(b) Continue the story in a way you think most suitable, until someone comes to relieve Alan. How long will he have to wait? How will he occupy himself?

Response

1   Write about a time when you have visited a sick relative at his or her home or in hospital and have been shocked by the difference between his or her normal healthy self and his or her present state.

2   Calming people down and putting them at their ease is not an easy thing to do. Write about a time when great tact and care was needed in order to reduce a build up of tension and restore a sense of calm and order once again.

31

Interruption at the OPERA HOUSE

by Brian Patten

At the very beginning of an important symphony,
while the rich and famous were settling into their quietly expensive
   boxes,

a man came crashing through the crowds,
5 carrying in his hand a cage in which
the rightful owner of the music sat,
yellow and tiny and very poor;
and taking onto the rostrum this rather timid bird
he turned up the microphones, and it sang.

10 'A very original beginning to the evening,' said the crowds,
quietly glancing at their programmes to find
the significance of the intrusion.

Meanwhile at the box office the organisers of the evening
were arranging for small and uniformed attendants
15 to evict, even forcefully, the intruders.
But as the attendants, poor and gathered from the nearby slums at
   little expense,

went rushing down the aisles to do their job
they heard, above the coughing and irritable rattling of jewels,

20 a sound that filled their heads with light,
and from somewhere inside them there bubbled up a stream,
and there came a breeze on which their youth was carried.
How sweetly the bird sang!

And though soon the fur-wrapped crowds
25 were leaving their boxes and in confusion were winding their way
   home

Interruption at the OPERA HOUSE

still the attendants sat in the aisles,
and some, so delighted at what they heard, rushed out to call
their families and friends.
30 And their children came,
sleepy for it was late in the evening,
very late in the evening,
and they hardly knew if they had done with dreaming
or had begun again.
35 In all the tenement blocks
the lights were clicking on,
and the rightful owner of the music,
tiny but no longer timid sang
for the rightful owners of the song.

Understanding

1 Suggest reasons for the differences between the way the audience responds to the interruption, the way the organisers of the event react and the way the attendants behave.

2 What aspects of the poem do you find the most difficult to believe? Give reasons for your answer.

3 Explain in your own words why the following phrases are important to the poem:
(a) 'the rightful owner of the music' (line 6)
(b) 'the coughing and irritable rattling of jewels' (line 19)
(c) 'a breeze on which their youth was carried.' (line 22)

4 What sense did you make of the ending to the poem, especially the last three lines?

5 Imagine you are a reporter for the local newspaper who was present at this event. Write a report of what happened at the opera house.

32

12 HOURS

by Adèle Geras

3.30 p.m. Friday afternoon. Early July.

She locked the front door behind her and walked to the corner of Marlowe Avenue trying very hard to look as though she were merely slipping out to the shops. You never knew who might be watching. She'd said so to Alex, and told him to wait for her round the corner.

As soon as she was in the car, as soon as the door was shut, Alex's arms were around her. He was kissing her. She was breathless, laughing, trembling.

'Not here, Alex,' she said. 'Someone could see . . .'

'So what? I love you. I want you . . . I'm going to shout it out of this window . . .' He began to wind it down.

'Stop it, Alex. I haven't breathed a word to Beth.'

'She must have guessed. I'm practically a fixture in your house.'

'Well, she knows you're a friend, of course she does, but . . .' Linda hesitated, '. . . she doesn't know the full extent.'

'Don't be so sure,' Alex said, and began to drive away. 'These teenagers know all about it. Every detail. Innocence is a thing of the past, I'm told.'

'But I'm her mother,' Linda said, sighing. 'You can imagine all kinds of things, but that's impossible . . . can you imagine *your* mother . . . ?'

Alex wrinkled his nose.

'The mind boggles.'

'Exactly.'

When Beth was born, she lay in a perspex cot: you could look through and see her tiny hands like pink sea creatures, waving above the cellular blanket. I lay in bed and stared at her for hours. It wasn't only love washing over me, it was a kind of terror. I thought then: this is what always and forever means. Every single thing she does from now until the moment of my death will be of the utmost importance to me. And it is. The most important thing.

4.00 p.m.

Beth Taylor rang the front door bell. There was no answer. Wearily she lifted the school bag off her shoulder and rooted around in one of the pockets for the back door key and walked around, and let herself in. This was not an unusual occurrence. Linda worked as a secretary in a school nearby, and never knew if the Head was going to pop in at half past three and tell her to type out a riveting letter about the spread of nits among the second year Juniors. Also, she sometimes had to shop on the way home. There was a note on the kitchen table.

'Dear Beth,

There's a meeting after school today, and then Alex and I are going to a movie and dinner. Sorry about this, but it only came up at lunchtime. Help yourself out of the freezer for your supper and do phone Pam or Rosie or Jean to visit you, but no orgiastic teenage parties, please!

See you later,

Love,

Mum.'

Beth swore under her breath, screwed up the note and threw it into a corner. Then she telephoned Pam.

'Come over after you've had supper,' she said. 'I'm all on my own. My mum's out gallivanting again.'

'Right,' said Pam. 'See you about seven thirty.'

Before the divorce, she was always there. That was the main thing about her: her constant presence. There always used to be a smell about the kitchen of cooking. Cakes and ratatouille mixed in with her smell, like old roses. I know, I know, said the poor distraught child, turning her tear-stained face away from the TV cameras, a Broken Home. How sad, how awful, how will I ever grow up to be anything other than a delinquent . . . but it wasn't like that. It was what they call a 'civilised divorce'. Everyone is still friends . . . or says they are. I still see my dad . . . nothing's really changed, because I never saw him much anyway. He was always away/abroad/busy, and now he's all those things still, only not in this house. The divorce didn't make much difference to me, but it changed Mum. She got a job, and she got a freezer and now bloody Alex, who's practically my age. Alex is O.K. I suppose. She

12 HOURS

could have told me a bit earlier, though. Prepared me. That's the trouble with grown-ups. No consideration for anyone else. Selfish.

5.00 p.m.

'Last time I skived off, I was twelve,' Linda said.

'What did you tell them?'

'That I was sick . . . that I'd be back O.K. on Monday.'

'And do you feel guilty?'

'Guilty as hell, but not on their account.'

Alex turned to look at her, and raised an eyebrow.

She said: 'It's Beth . . . how do you think she'd feel if she knew her mother'd been making love half the afternoon? It's naughty.'

'But nice. Like the cream cakes. Come here.'

Linda moved into the curve of Alex's arm and closed her eyes.

After Clive left, I thought I'd never feel anything again. Then Alex came to the school, and the very first time I saw him, I grew soft all over. For ages I just looked at him whenever I got the chance and wanted him like mad. I was like a kid, stupid and tongue-tied, rushing down certain corridors, going home down certain streets in the hope of bumping into him. I couldn't believe, still can hardly believe, that he felt what he said he felt. The first time he kissed me, behind the door of the stationery room (what a cliché!) I blushed and nearly fainted, like a young girl, weak under his hands. Now when I'm with him, it's like being drunk: it's heat and light and I have no control over myself. I'm not behaving in a grown-up fashion. He's ten years younger than I am. His skin is smooth like a small child's. When I'm with him, he's all I can think about. I've tried to be discreet at school, but I feel like a Ready Brek advertisement, glowing all over, all the time.

7.45 p.m.

'I think,' said Pam, 'that he's quite fanciable, from what I've seen.'

'He's all right, I suppose,' said Beth, 'if you like the doomed poet type: all floppy blond hair and long fingers.'

'I wouldn't say no.'

'I would,' said Beth. 'I think there's altogether too much sex about. I don't reckon it's good for you.'

'Rubbish. Who said so?'

'I've read all about it.' Beth held up her hand and ticked the points off, one by one. 'First off, you can get pregnant. Then, if you go on the pill, your hormones get mucked about, then you can get herpes and stuff like that, and then they say you can get cancer of the cervix from it. Seems a bit bloody hazardous to me.'

'When you're in love,' Pam said, 'you don't think about all that. You get carried away.'

'I call that,' Beth said, 'irresponsible. She's my mum. She's got no right to get carried away . . . she's got me to think of, hasn't she?'

'But she isn't fifteen, is she? All those things you mentioned are only supposed to happen to people our age, not to mums. Probably grown-up propaganda to stop us having fun.'

'I don't know about fun so much . . . it sounds a bit messy and revolting to me.'

'It's all different when you're in love,' Pam said firmly.

'But how on earth are you meant to know when you *are* in love?' Beth sighed.

Pam pondered this question for a moment. 'You know you're in love,' she said finally, 'when all that stuff *doesn't* seem messy and revolting any more.' She looked at her watch. 'Isn't it time for that movie on telly?'

She's changed, there's no doubt about that. Her clothes are different. Well, before she only ever stood about the house and did housework, or dug in the garden, so jeans and a baggy old sweater were O.K. Now she has to have decent clothes for school, I understand that, but I don't just mean her clothes . . . she's had her ears pierced, and wears long earrings that catch the light, and she's changed her perfume. It's not soft pink roses any more. It's a brown, smooth, thick smell, like fur. Perhaps Alex gave it to her. She wears blusher. I caught her putting on her make-up the other day . . . her bra was pink and lacy and her bosom seemed to be slipping out over the top. Her knickers were like tiny little lace-trimmed shorts . . . I asked her about them and she said they were new and did I like them, but she was blushing like crazy, all the way down her neck, and she dressed very quickly after that . . . that was when I began to suspect about Alex. There's a couple writhing around on telly this very minute. If I think of Alex and Mum doing that, I feel quite ill. I wonder if Pam really likes this film . . . I wouldn't mind turning over to another channel.

2.30 a.m.

Linda leapt out of bed.

'Alex! Alex, wake up, for heaven's sake! Look at the time . . . it'll be morning at this rate before I get home. Come on, Alex, please, wake up! Beth'll be worried frantic . . . please.'

Alex yawned and stretched and smiled.

12 HOURS

'Relax. It's O.K. I'm awake now. I'll be ready in two shakes of a lamb's tail. And don't worry about Beth. She's a big girl. She'll have gone to sleep hours ago.'

'Please hurry, Alex.' Linda sighed. 'I knew we shouldn't have come back here for coffee after dinner. I knew at the time it was a mistake.'

'No, you didn't. You couldn't wait, go on, admit it . . .'

'I admit it, I admit it, now for the last time, will you get your bloody shoes on, and let's get out of here!'

I wish he could drive faster. I wish we could be home sooner. Oh, please, let Beth be O.K. Let her not be worried. Let the house not have burned to the ground, let there not be a mad axeman on the loose. Please, please, don't let me be punished. I know I shouldn't have gone back for coffee, but please let it be all right and I'll never do it again. It's just that every second since she was born I've thought about every one of my actions in relation to her. Will Beth be O.K.? Want to go to the hairdresser? Then fix someone to pick her up from school. Want to go to the movies? Find a babysitter. Beth twenty minutes late back from school? All kinds of horrors flying behind the eyes. Now that she's a little older, nearly a grown-up, I feel as though I'm able to do certain things without looking over my shoulder to make sure she's all right. But not everything. Please, Beth, be all right. Don't be angry. Please understand.

3.30 a.m.

'Mum, is that you?'

'Ssh. Yes it's me. Are you O.K.?' Whispering.

'You don't need to whisper. I'm not asleep.'

Linda came into Beth's room and sat on the bed. 'Haven't you been asleep at all?'

'Oh, yes, on and off. In between worrying myself sick about you . . . where the hell have you been? It's bloody half past three in the morning.'

'Oh, Bethy, my love, I'm so sorry. I was having such a good time . . . I just forgot about the time . . . I'm really sorry. I won't do it again, I promise.'

'I thought you might have had a car crash . . . you could have rung up, couldn't you, when you knew you'd be late. Couldn't you? And what are you giggling about?'

Linda had started to laugh, and now, weak from lack of sleep and relief that Beth was there, just the same under her flower-printed

144

sheets, her laughter grew and grew until the tears were streaming down her cheeks.

'You should hear yourself . . . you sound like a mother, you do honestly, and me . . . I feel like a juvenile delinquent.'

'Delinquent . . . yes. Juvenile . . . I'm not quite so sure . . .' Beth, happy to have her mother home again, even wearing new perfume, began to laugh as well.

It's like one of those books where someone wakes up one day and she's turned into someone else. Or when a family discovers their child is really a mouse or something. There's a famous one where a guy wakes up and finds he's become this huge cockroach-type creature . . . you can see someone's point of view much better from another perspective. I always used to get dead irritated when I'd come home late and see Mum peering down the road, all white-faced and frowny, but I know how she feels now. She wasn't at the movies till 3.30. She must be sleeping with Alex. That'll take some getting used to. I must get used to it. I will.

Understanding

1   There are six timed entries which make up this story. Each entry seems to consist of two quite different pieces: a 'narrative' section and a 'perspectives' section. Draw up a simple grid based on the six times given by the entries. Underneath each time, name the main participant in the 'narrative' piece, then name the person responsible for the 'voice' behind the second, 'perspectives' piece. Your grid will look like this:

Time

Main participant
in 'narrative'

whose Voice
in 'perspectives'

2   Now that you have looked closely at the shape of this short story, how would you describe the differences between the two 'sections' used throughout? Looking up the words 'narrative' and 'perspective' in a dictionary may help, but rely mainly on your own understanding of the differences involved. Describe as many differences as you can find.

the little pet...

5   Many readers feel puzzled about why the boy feels so
    sympathetic to the rabbit at the end of the story. There
    might be no 'correct' answer here, but what are your views?

6   The title of the story is 'The Little Pet'. Now that you have
    read and considered the whole story, why do you think the
    writer chose that particular title?

7   Either:
    (a) Imagine a situation where Martha and Francis senior
    find an injured fledgeling fallen from a nest. Write the story
    in which Francis junior discovers them attempting to deal
    with it. Base your writing on evidence found in the story.
    Or:
    (b) Put yourself in Francis junior's shoes and describe your
    thoughts and reactions as the two parents play their games
    with the rabbit (lines 49–68). What would be running
    through your mind?

Response

1   Think back to times when you have been talked down to by
    adults. Then write a comic scene where anxious parents like
    Martha and Francis senior try to explain to their son or
    daughter where babies come from, or other similar ideas.

2   The novelty of looking after a pet soon wears off! Write an
    imaginary journal or diary recording precisely how your
    relationship with a pet changes over a week or a month.

12 HOURS

3　At the end of the story, the point is made that 'you can see someone's point of view much better from another perspective'. In the case of this story, do you feel that the presence of other 'perspectives' has helped or hindered your understanding of what was going on? Give reasons for your answer.

4　From the four statements below, select the one with which you most strongly agree and the one with which you most strongly disagree. Also write down the reasons behind your selections.

- This is a disgraceful story which has no place in schools at any level.
- This is a provocative story which forces a reader to reflect on important contemporary questions.
- This is an interesting story for some of the time but there were parts I did not really understand.
- This is a silly story which did not move me one way or the other.

5　Either:
(a) Re-read the entry for 2.30 a.m. The first 'narrative' section involves both Alex and Linda, yet the second, 'perspectives' piece contains only Linda's point of view. Write a further 'perspectives' piece which would express the thoughts and perceptions of Alex.
Or:
(b) The next entry would be sometime the following morning, a Saturday. Choose a suitable time and then write out your own twin-sectioned entry by choosing who you want to involve in your 'narrative' and 'perspectives' pieces.

Response

1　Write about a time when your feelings of loyalty or responsibility to someone have prevented you from doing something you would really like to have done.

2　Sometimes parents can be the most difficult people to confide in. Write about a situation where a son or a daughter desperately wants to talk to a parent but something, fear, embarrassment or whatever, holds him or her back.

the little pet... by Dan Jacobson

They put the rabbit hutch at the bottom of the garden, in a sheltered position between the back fence and a bank of tall lupins that grew across the bottom of the lawn. The weather was warm and summery, and it had been like that for weeks, with only an occasional
5 thundercloud passing overhead at night and letting fall a little rain, so that their enclosed little back-garden was heavy every morning with the smell of growth and bright with the glittering of water on grass. And into the leafy, clean-smelling corner went the rabbit hutch, and the pregnant rabbit within it.
10   'Poor thing, she doesn't know what's happening to her.'
     Martha kneeled on the ground to have a closer look at the rabbit and her husband leaned over her, propping himself on a corner of the hutch with one hand. His movements were all quick and angular, and he made too many of them; the eye of an onlooker might have been
15 tempted to skip the lightly dressed, light-coloured husband, and rest on the wife. She could comfortably have taken the scrutiny, for she was small and dark and pretty enough, with her broad brow and wide brown eyes. But she too — like her husband — had the strained and guilty air of the perpetually well-intentioned. It was their laugh that
20 betrayed them: only two people who had lived together for some years and were very keen on meeting each other at all points could have laughed so much like each other. It was a practised, accommo-dating, nervous laugh that they both had, a laugh that never lasted long but was always quick to come again, with a rattle in their throats
25 and a chatter between their teeth. It was a pity that little Francis, their only son, who was standing silently by, did not join in their laughter too.
     'She'll soon get used to being here,' Martha said to the boy, 'and then you'll be able to play with her.'
30   'Yes,' the little boy said.
     'You'll love playing with her,' Martha said.
     'Yes,' the little boy said.

the little pet...

'Oh, see what she's doing now,' Francis senior said. He and
Martha were standing arm-in-arm, so he could easily wheel her
round to see. The boy stepped forward carefully to see too, and his
parents, together, made way for him, grateful for the interest he was
showing. The rabbit had been bought for him, after all, and they let
him stand in front of them and look. They could see easily enough,
over his head.

The rabbit had been bought for little Francis, and how the
parents worked in the next few weeks at the fun that the rabbit was
going to provide him. How assiduously they cleaned out the hutch
every day and saw to it that there was fresh water for the rabbit to
drink and fresh grass for the rabbit to lie on. When it rained they
brought the hutch into the kitchen and kept it there, though it was
quite a job for Francis to bring the clumsy contraption of wood and
wire netting through the door without scratching the paint on the
doorposts, and Martha found it very much in the way when she was
cooking. They fed the rabbit lettuce and carrots and cabbage leaves,
even though carrots, particularly, were dishearteningly expensive
that season. And they watched the rabbit, talked to the rabbit, put
their fingers through the wire and waved them at the rabbit, tried to
get the rabbit to answer their calls, invented names for the rabbit,
discarded these names and invented better ones. They said the rabbit
looked like a grandmother, so they called it Granny; they said the
rabbit looked like the villain in a Western, so they called it Pardner;
sometimes it simply looked sweet, they said, like a bunny that had
something to do with an Easter egg or a cold little bunny on a
Christmas card, and then they admitted, laughing rapidly and leaning
against one another, that they didn't know what they should call it
except a darling of a bunny br'er rabbit. And to this joy they added the
joy of thinking of names for the little ones the rabbit was at any time
due to have. Irresponsibly they prophesied that the rabbit would
have at least seven little bunnies, at least ten little bunnies, twenty.

'What'll we do if it has twenty?' Francis asked, mockingly aghast.

'We'll declare it a public holiday,' Martha replied. And then to
the little boy: 'Wouldn't you like twenty little bunnies to play with?
What a lot of bunnies.'

'Do rabbits ever have twenty babies?' the boy asked.

The parents looked at one another, and their laugh went no
lower than their throats. 'I don't think we know.'

'Then why did you say it will?'

'We didn't say it will, darling. We were just hoping. Wouldn't you
like twenty little bunnies to play with?'

75　　　Little Francis considered carefully for a moment before he flatly replied, 'Yes.' His watchfulness upset his parents; they had hoped that more of it would have been directed upon the rabbit and less of it upon themselves.

　　　But they persisted. They persisted with the rabbit even though
80　the rabbit was no more responsive to their humour than their son. The rabbit never really looked like a grandmother or a villain in a Western or a bunny on a Christmas card, and it never responded to their names and their games: the rabbit ate the food they gave it and went about its rabbity business in the little space it had. Loudly and
85　laughingly, Martha and Francis insisted on how very amusing it was to have a rabbit in their back garden, how cleverly the rabbit's ears moved, how handsomely its fur lay, how intelligent its eyes were — but neither of them was keen on actually handling the rabbit, for fear of fleas, and even for fear of being bitten, for the rabbit had the look of
90　a rabbit that would bite if it felt like it.

　　　And really Martha and Francis could not help thinking sometimes, a rabbit was a strange-looking animal. Its face was so strange, with that squared, prominent shape of the central bone, cut sharply downwards, almost hammer-like like one of those sledge-hammers
95　that men use to break rocks. And then, a long way below the eyes, below the crown of that hammerlike bone, there was the rest of the face: the flat, almost indistinguishable nose, with the rifts of the nostrils concealed unless they were active; and below that secretive nose the mouth, with its upper lip that split so horribly in two when the
100　animal ate, revealing shamelessly pink flesh, gaping like some kind of wound. While above all mysteriously independent of the rest, the tall ears swung forward or lay back flat or half-turned, pivoting in some crafty hollow in the skull. The rabbit was black in colour, but not entirely, for many of the hairs were tipped at the end with a strange
105　rusty colour, a kind of red, the colour of dried blood. These tips glowed, when they caught the sunlight, so that the crouching animal looked like a drop that would be scorching to hold in the hand — a little ball of fire for which Martha and Francis had too lightly assumed responsibility. But when the sun was gone from it, the rabbit in its
110　hutch looked no more than nondescript, rusty. Only its eyes were bright and mobile then, though sometimes the whiskers and half-secret nostrils would tremble with apprehensions that Martha's or Francis's grosser faculties could not respond to, in their green garden, behind the fence of palings.

115　The catastrophes with the rabbit came quickly upon one another, the second within a day of the first. When the rabbit finally gave birth Francis came down one morning and found one tiny mouse-like creature crawling blindly round its mother. It had grey fur, still darkly

the little pet...

matted, and it seemed quite blind, and the mother rabbit showed no
120   interest in it. Confidently the adults prophesied to one another that
during the day it would give birth to more, to more than one; but in
the evening when Francis came back from work it was to find that no
more little rabbits had been produced. 'She's hiding the little one,'
Martha said. 'She hasn't moved.'
125   'How is the little one?'
'I don't know,' Martha said. 'I've only seen it once, and it looked
so feeble. Do you know what a little rabbit is supposed to look like?'
she asked her husband. 'This one looks so awful, like a kind of worm.
Are they supposed to be blind? Like kittens — kittens are born blind,
130   aren't they?'
Francis laughed but his wife did not join him. 'And little Francis?'
he asked.
'He's in the garden. He's playing. I haven't seen him watching
her much.'
135   'And he wouldn't have seen much if he had been watching her?'
'No.'
'One little rabbit. I hope Francis doesn't remember what we
promised him.'
'I hope the little rabbit is all right.'
140   'Oh, it is,' Francis assured his wife.
When Francis went out before supper the little rabbit was hidden
under its mother. Francis junior was playing quietly in the garden; he
was as quiet as ever, and as neat, with the comb-marks in his hair still
showing from where his mother had combed it after lunch. He too
145   told his father that he hadn't seen the little rabbit since the morning.
The next morning, when Francis came down early to make the
coffee and put on the toast, there was still no sign of the little rabbit.
But Martha's first question on waking had been about the little one,
and disturbed as he was by his wife's anxiety, Francis was determined
150   now to see it — to see if it were really the grey, blind bundle of feeble
movement that he remembered it to be. He tempted the mother
rabbit forward with some wet grass that he plucked at his feet, but she
did not move; he went back into the kitchen and brought some
lettuce leaves out of the larder and offered them to her, but still she
155   did not move. He snapped his fingers, he called her — not by any of
the names they had given her, but simply saying, 'Come here, come
here,' but she did not come forward. So in a petulant little anger he
pulled out a cane from one of the flower-beds and prodded her with
it. The cane slid for a moment on the rabbit's close-packed fur and the
160   loose skin beneath, before it found a hold on the haunch. Francis

jabbed, he struck upwards, and the rabbit slowly came forward. Francis stared, with the stick in his hand. There was nothing under the rabbit.

He stared, and for a moment he turned and looked up at the window of the bedroom where Francis junior slept. Had the boy taken the little rabbit out? Had Martha? But that was madness, and his heels slipped on the wet grass as he turned and stared again at the point of his stick, where the little rabbit should have been. There was nothing there.

Then Francis saw that there was something there. There were a few hairs and a few droppings, but Francis gingerly moved the stick past these, and carefully turned over a small ball of hair, and saw the dark clots of blood within it, and in the next that he turned over, and the last. They were all that was left of the little rabbit.

Francis dropped his stick. 'Martha!' he shouted. 'Martha!' He met her in the kitchen, and together they rushed to inspect what Francis had told her of. But they had time only to stare for a moment into the hutch before Francis junior appeared through the kitchen door. 'He mustn't see it,' Martha said. 'He mustn't know. Take him away, Francis, quickly!'

'Breakfast,' Francis cheerfully called and picked up the little boy and carried him back indoors, with Martha following them both. While she was giving little Francis his breakfast, the father went outside and cleared up the mess. He did not speak to the mother-rabbit, nor did he look at her. Only once, when she got in his way, did he give her a fierce unwarranted jab in the ribs with the garden trowel he was using for the job.

After breakfast the little boy was sent into the garden, and then Martha, who had been very calm and stiff during breakfast, fell upon her husband. 'I will not have that animal in my house for another single day. I can't bear it. I don't want it. You must take it to the pet-shop at once.'

'But darling, I'll be late for work.'

'I don't care if you'll be late for work. You must take it away. I will not have it here.' Martha was small and fierce, like a little fighter, and Francis could not argue with her.

'All right, darling,' he said. 'I'll take it in the car.'

'Do it at once.'

'All right, darling.'

He went to the garden, and for the last time picked up the clumsy hutch. But little Francis followed him.

'Where are you taking it? Where are you taking the bunny?'

the little pet...

'Back to the pet-shop.'

'Why?'

205   'He has to, darling,' Martha said. 'The bunny's sick.'

'No it's not,' the boy said, turning to his mother. He was dressed, as always, with great neatness, in a white T-shirt and a pair of khaki shorts; he was not a boy whose features anyone remembered particularly, but Martha saw to it that his clothes were always spotless.

210   'It is sick, darling.'

'No it's not.'

If Martha had not been so upset she would simply have ordered her husband to get on with what he was doing. But now she brought her hands to her mouth and from behind her knuckles she asked,

215   'Francis, do you know why we're taking the bunny to the pet-shop?'

'Yes,' the child replied.

Martha half-dropped one hand, the other remaining at her mouth. And Francis senior could not move, though he stood with his arms spreadeagled, carrying the hutch. Then Martha moved,

220   grabbing the child by the wrist.

'Why?' she demanded, and shook his arm. 'Why?'

'I think it's because she killed the little bunny.'

'So you KNOW!' Martha shrieked.

'Yes.'

225   'And you didn't say anything about it!' The parents looked with horror at their child. But he met their gaze.

When eventually he spoke he did not seem to be in any way excusing himself. Rather he seemed to want to help his parents by explaining, 'I saw the little bits.'

230   'Francis!' Martha exclaimed. Francis senior could say nothing. He could only put the hutch down, and sit on it, and get his arms akimbo. Underneath him the disturbed rabbit was scurrying as if seeking for foothold.

Then Martha bent towards the child again. 'But why didn't you

235   tell us?'

The child looked down at the hutch. 'Because I thought you'd take the bunny away if I told you.'

Francis senior spoke at last, with a jerk of his head and a jerk of his arms. 'And you're right. We aren't having it here for another day.'

240   Then to silence the scurrying rabbit he gave a vicious little back-kick at the hutch beneath him. The scurrying increased in violence.

'There you are,' said the little boy.

He seemed acquiescent enough, but Martha straightened herself and moved to her husband, and took him by the arm.

245 'Wait,'she said, and at the tone of her voice Francis rose to meet her,
and the husband and wife stood closely together. 'Francis,' Martha
said softly, as if the word she had to speak might break in her mouth if
she said it carelessly, 'do you love the bunny?'

She could not meet the clear grey stare the child gave her. He
250 looked straight at her, and did not open his mouth to answer her
question, like someone who would not admit that he knew the
meaning of the word.

And Martha dropped her husband's arm and began to walk
away. 'Let it stay,' she said. 'Let him have it.'
255 'But —'

'Let it stay,' Martha said from a few yards off, without looking
back, still walking towards the kitchen.

'All right then,' Francis senior said, giving the hutch a parting
kick. 'But you'll have to feed it and give it water and everything else.'
260 He began to walk after his wife. He left the hutch in the middle of their
lawn.

'Yes,' the little boy said.

He waited until his father had gone into the house, then he went
on his knees in front of the hutch. He put his fingers through the wire
265 netting. 'Come here,' he said to the rabbit. 'I'm not cross with you. I
knew you didn't like your baby.'

Understanding

1   What do you learn about Martha and Francis senior as
    characters from the opening section of the story when they
    are settling in the rabbit? Read up to line 145, paying
    particular attention to the things they say and do, and use
    this information as evidence to support your answer.

2   Looking closely at the story from the beginning to line 211,
    what are your first impressions of Francis junior?
    Remember to support the points you make with evidence
    from the story.

3   The feelings of Francis senior and Martha towards the rabbit
    seem to change as the story goes on. How and why do their
    feelings change, in your opinion?

4   Do you think the parents love Francis junior? If so why do
    you think that? If not, try to say exactly what they do feel for
    him.

Remember
by Alice Walker

Remember me?
I am the girl
with the dark skin
whose shoes are thin
I am the girl
with rotted teeth
I am the dark
rotten-toothed girl
with the wounded eye
and the melted ear.

I am the girl
holding their babies
cooking their meals
sweeping their yards
washing their clothes
Dark and rotting
and wounded, wounded.

I would give
to the human race
only hope.

I am the woman
with the blessed
dark skin
I am the woman
with teeth repaired
I am the woman
with the healing eye
the ear that hears.

I am the woman: Dark,
repaired, healed
Listening to you.

I would give
to the human race
only hope.

Remember

I am the woman
offering two flowers
whose roots
are twin

Justice and Hope

Let us begin.

Understanding

1   After reading the whole poem through several times, read verse one again, carefully. What are your first impressions of the girl in this poem? Who is she? What might her circumstances be?

2   In verse two, who, in your opinion, are 'they'? Give as many reasons for your answer as you can.

3   The short verse three seems to act as a 'hinge' to the whole poem. After those three lines, many things start to change. How would you describe the changes that are mentioned in verse four?

4   The pattern of the verses also change here and a number of shorter verses follow. Verse five includes the line 'Listening to you.' Who do you think she is listening to at this point in the poem?

5   Finally, the woman offers two flowers whose roots are 'Justice and Hope' before ending with the request, 'Let us begin.' How do you respond to this request? Begin what? How does your response connect with your thoughts and feelings on the poem as a whole?

Response

1   The poem starts with a girl's voice and then moves on to a woman's. More time has passed. The same woman is now much older. She starts to look back on her life and her earlier hopes. Using a similar style to that found in the original poem, write down her thoughts as she looks back and remembers for a second time.

Answers see pages 12, 21, 49 and 55

When I was 15
Michael Rosen

Ken said to me,
'You know your trouble,
you don't hold your bag right.'
'What's wrong with it?' I said.
'It's not so much the way you
    hold it —
It's the way you put it down.
You've got to look at it as if you
    hate it.
Watch me.'

He went out
he walked back in
shoulders back
elbows out
bag balanced in his hand.

'Watch me.'

He stopped walking.
His arm froze
and the bag flew out of his hand
as if he'd kicked it.
He didn't even look at it.
'Now you try,' he said.
'I'll show you where you've gone
    wrong.'
I went out the door,
I rambled back in again with my
    bag.
I stopped walking
My arm froze — just like his,
but the bag fell out of my hand
and flopped on to the floor
like a fried egg.

'Useless,' he said.
'You don't convince — that's your
    trouble.'
'So?' I said.
'I'm a slob. I can't change that.'
I didn't say that I *would* try and
    change
in case that would show I was giving
    in to him.
But secretly
on my own,
in my room,
in front of the mirror
I spent hours and hours
practising bag-dropping.
Walking in,
freeze the arm,
let the bag drop.
Walk in
arm freeze
bag drop.
Again and again
till I thought I had got it right.

I don't suppose any girl noticed.
I don't suppose any girl ever said to
    herself,
'I love the way he drops his bag . . .'

Robot on the Rampage

James Morrow and Murray Suid

INTERIOR LIGHTHOUSE — MID-SHOT — DAY

5. The keeper is standing by his pantry, holding empty food containers.

KEEPER
My throat is parched . . . already hunger gnaws at me! There is not a bit of food left in here! What can I do? What —??

EXTERIOR LIGHTHOUSE — MID-SHOT — DAY

6. A tighter shot of the robot sitting on box, as in Shot 4.

ROBOT
I am waiting, mortal! I shall *always* wait! Time means nothing to me! You are doomed!

INTERIOR LIGHTHOUSE — MID-SHOT — DAY

7. A slight high-angle of the keeper, who is in the foreground, facing the camera. The robot can be seen through the window, sitting on the ground.

KEEPER (voice-over)
He's been out there for days . . . I can't hold out any longer . . . I've got to have food . . . water . . . there is *one* chance for me . . . one slim chance . . .

EXTERIOR LIGHTHOUSE — FULL SHOT — DAY

8. Jump cut to the keeper coming out the lighthouse door, taken over the robot's shoulder. Robot is still sitting.

ROBOT
I *knew* you'd come, mortal! No human can defeat a superior *robot!*

EXTERIOR LIGHTHOUSE — CLOSE-UP — DAY

9. Cut to reverse angle of robot, still sitting.

ROBOT
You humans made one mistake when you built us . . . you made us capable of living without food . . . without water . . . without sleep! We need *nothing* to keep us alive! That is why I can easily outwait you!

EXTERIOR LIGHTHOUSE — EXTREME LONG-SHOT — DAY

10. Keeper and robot face each other, lighthouse in background.

ROBOT
And now . . . you shall watch me extinguish the light . . . you will see the sinking of the 'Superba' . . . and then you will meet your *own* fate! I have spoken!

EXTERIOR LIGHTHOUSE — MID-SHOT — DAY

11. Tighter on the robot, slight low-angle.

ROBOT
But . . . wait! What is wrong? I — I am powerless to *move*! I — I am helpless! My limbs do not function!

EXTERIOR LIGHTHOUSE — MID-SHOT — DAY

12. Robot stares into camera.

ROBOT
Why? How? What has *happened* to me?

EXTERIOR LIGHTHOUSE — MID-SHOT — DAY

13. Two-shot of robot and keeper, slight low-angle.

KEEPER
I gambled on *one* thing, pal, and it paid off! If I could keep you sitting out here long enough . . .

EXTERIOR LIGHTHOUSE — EXTREME LONG-SHOT — DAY

14. The camera is so far away we can see the lighthouse surrounded by water. The keeper and the robot are barely visible.

KEEPER
. . . in the salt air, with the sea spray and the dampness, I had a hunch you would *rust solid!* And you did! So just *sit* there, robot, while I send for help! Your type will *never* be superior to humans — because you were made by *us* — but *we* were created by someone vastly *greater!* Think about that, *robot* . . . think about it untii — the end!
(fade out)

THE END

After a Quarrel
John Richmond

She sat on a bench in the freezing night, in the rain.
He stood a hundred yards away, and watched her back.
They had cursed, driven the last oaths in the language
Into one another's brain.
Now one dilemma faced them both;
How to step across the concrete, forgive, be forgiven,
Get in the warm again, but not do it first.

Gregory's Girl — the Cookery Class
Bill Forsyth, Andrew Bethell and Gerald Cole

GREGORY Come on! I mean Dorothy, she came into the team last week. She's in 4A . . . she's a wonderful player, she's a *girl*. She goes around with Carol and Susan, she's got long lovely hair, she always looks really clean and fresh, and she smells mmm . . . lovely. Even if you just pass her in the corridor she smells, mmm, gorgeous . . . She's got teeth, lovely teeth, lovely white, white teeth . . .

STEVE Oh, *that* Dorothy, the hair . . . the smell . . . the teeth . . . *that* Dorothy.

GREGORY That's her, that's Dorothy.

STEVE The one that took your place in the team.

GREGORY So what. She's a good footballer. She might be a bit light but she's got skill, she's some girl . . .

STEVE Can she cook? Can she do this?

(Steve throws the rolled out pastry into the air and juggles it with a pizza-maker's flourish.)

GREGORY (*Being very serious*) When you're in love, things like that just don't matter.

STEVE Gimme the margarine.

GREGORY Do you think she'll love me back?

STEVE No chance . . . watch that mix! I told you, nice and slowly . . . take it easy . . . (*Steve takes Gregory's hands in his and guides him through the movements of a nice and easy stir.*)

GREGORY What d'you mean no chance?

STEVE No chance.